A Biography of
Distinguished Scientist
Gilbert Newton Lewis

Front cover photo:
Gilbert Newton Lewis

A BIOGRAPHY OF DISTINGUISHED SCIENTIST
Gilbert Newton Lewis

Edward S. Lewis
His Son

The Edwin Mellen Press
Lewiston•Queenston•Lampeter

Library of Congress Cataloging-in-Publication Data

Lewis, Edward S., 1920-
  A biography of distinguished scientist Gilbert Newton Lewis /
Edward S. Lewis.
    p. cm.
  Includes bibliographical references and index.
  ISBN 0-7734-8284-9 (hardcover)
  1. Lewis, Gilbert Newton, 1875-1946. 2. Chemists--United States-
-Biography.   I. Title.
QD22.L57L48   1998
540'.92--dc21   98-25084
[B]   CIP

A CIP catalog record for this book is available from the British Library.

The Edwin Mellen Press   The Edwin Mellen Press
Box 450   Box 67
Lewiston, New York   Queenston, Ontario
USA 14092-0450   CANADA L0S 1L0

The Edwin Mellen Press, Ltd.
Lampeter, Ceredigion, Wales
UNITED KINGDOM SA48 8LT

Printed in the United States of America

This book is dedicated to the grandchildren of Gilbert N. Lewis in the hope that they will learn something more about their illustrious grandfather's distinction: Sylvia, David, Jerry, Gil, Cynny, Arthur, Rich and Aki.

TABLE OF CONTENTS

Acknowledgement   i

Foreword   iii

Introduction   1

Chapter I   Lewis's Life and Career Up to 1912   5

Chapter II   Publications Through 1912   15

Chapter III   The Berkeley and California Environment   19

Chapter IV   Career 1912 to 1946   23

Chapter V   The Department   27

Chapter VI   Publications and Research From 1913 On   29

Chapter VII   Lewis as Administrator   51

Chapter VIII   The Research Conference   55

Chapter IX   The Nobel Prize?   61

Chapter X   Lewis, Lachman, Conversation and Cards   67

Chapter XI   Lewis as Family Man   71

Chapter XII   The Las Vegas Symposium   87

Chapter XIII   Lewis as a Person   89

Chapter XIV   Paretchan and Letters from Nobel Winners   93

References   103

Index   115

Acknowledgement

The help of many people has been essential. These include the original prodding by Prof. Seaborg, the continued interest of Harold Paretchan, my nephew Gilbert Newton Lewis (Gil), who looked at the manuscript in an early version and offered many suggestions, and who collected a number of old photographs and provided background for most. My sister Margery Selby also contributed a number of family snapshots, a collection of reprints and several oral recollections. My niece Cynthia Shaffer also contributed photographs. Special thanks are due to my son, Richard P. Lewis for skillfully converting many faded photographs for which negatives were unavailable into respectable publication-worthy prints.

Foreword

Gilbert N. Lewis was an extraordinary and world-renown scientist, and also my father. To write a biography requires making an impossible decision. On the one hand, to do his chemistry justice would need an analysis of his 168 published papers set in the period of his time, identifying those which blazed new trails, as well as those which have come to naught. Such an effort would leave the average nonscientific reader bored, and would leave his personality a mystery. Describing his origins, his life, and his family life as I remember it would overlook his distinction as a scientist.

I take an intermediate position in this informal biography. His life and ancestry are covered in a way that is, by historical standards, inadequate, and it is combined with an account, without analysis, of some of his most important scientific work, including the development of a research spirit in the department that is his most lasting legacy. To this are added some high points of my memories of him as father and the head of his family. I hope that the nonscientist reader will not quit before leaving the science and go on to his ancestry, his education, his ideas about the education of his children, and other more personal characteristics. The influence he had on his colleagues and on the whole department comes from a blend of his science and his personality. I present this influence as a reality, but also as an amazing accomplishment.

Introduction

Gilbert Newton Lewis, an illustrious and distinguished chemist and scientist was chairman of the chemistry department and dean of the College of Chemistry at the University of California for nearly thirty years until five years before his death in 1946. He published his first paper in 1898, and his last posthumous paper appeared in 1949. Thus his scientific work almost coincided with the first half of the twentieth century. That period included great changes not only in science, but in society. It included the development of effective broadcast radio, the beginning of broadcast television, the beginning of the experiment of communism as a governmental system. It included the great depression and two world wars. The development of electronics, spurred by the invention of the vacuum tube has had enormous consequences, with great military applications. Computers were in their infancy in the very late forties, automobiles were just a curiosity at the beginning of the century and started their advance to the level of an ubiquitous nuisance and necessity by the end of this period. The discovery of uranium fission and its consequence nuclear power (initially as the atomic bomb) was the most striking scientific and political development of the period, but many scientists would point out that this period also included the birth and development of quantum mechanics and of the theory of relativity. A vital part of the practical development of the isolation, purification and development of a practical plant for the new element plutonium was carried out during the war by members of the chemistry and physics departments of the University of California. In biology, the identification of genetic material as DNA had just been made, but the extraordinary ramifications of this discovery in terms of structure and function were still in the future.

G. N. Lewis was born in 1875, he died in 1946, and the extraordinary career in between is hardly matched in this century. In 1994, Glenn Seaborg, one of his collaborators and colleagues, suggested to me that it would be a good idea to have someone write a biography. Since Lewis was my father as well as a distinguished physical chemist, I concurred. However, nothing happened except that I continued to think about it. The question of who could undertake such a biography was a puzzle, for few of his contemporaries were still alive.

I decided to look into the Lewis archives in the University of California Library, and a previously planned trip in the summer of 1995 to the west to visit my son Richard in Seattle and my sister Margery in Berkeley seemed like a good opportunity to do this. I therefore contacted the archive librarian and Professor Seaborg. Richard and I then met with Seaborg, who reiterated his interest in a biography, and Richard and I went to see the archives. I promised to collect some information from a variety of sources to use as a basis for a biography. In the course of this I realized that I was the obvious choice for the biographer, even though lacking any previous experience at such writing.

A biography is usually written by someone who has access to written or oral descriptions of the biographee's life and work with the factual part of the work being documented thoroughly so that it can be checked against these original documents. Alternatively, a biography can be written by someone with a personal acquaintance of the subject with the writer's memory and personal papers being the source of the information. I undertook this task from a compromise position. Lewis was 45 when I was born and I can not claim to much personal information for the early years. Thus for about the first fifty years of his life, I must rely mainly on family stories, the printed record, and very little oral memory from others, since he has now been dead for half a century. There are very few friends or colleagues alive to give me private unpublished material. A symposium organized by Derek Davenport at the 1982 ACS meeting in Las Vegas did however include three colleagues (Calvin, Pitzer and Seaborg), one faculty member who was a graduate student in the Lewis era (Brewer), two PhD students (Bigeleisen and Kasha), an old associate and friend (Pauling), my brother Richard Lewis, and three science historians (Jensen, Servos and Stranges); all had recollections and discussions shedding much light on Lewis, the science he had done and his approach to research.

This 1982 symposium entitled "Gilbert Newton Lewis 1875-1946" was a major source of information. These talks were published in *The Journal of Chemical Education* in the first three issues of 1984. Unfortunately I was not able to hear these talks when presented because of a sudden illness lasting throughout the meeting and have had to rely entirely on the written versions. I have no reason to believe that these differ substantially from the spoken presentations.

There are a number of sources of information about Lewis and his life; I had hoped that the Lewis archives in the Bancroft Library in Berkeley would be especially useful. This turned out to be rather disappointing, among the contents were letters to Lewis from many sources, but almost all of Lewis's side of the correspondence is not there, perhaps due to the nuisance of carbon paper and the absence of copy machines which in a newer archive would have led to a more complete record. In addition to these letters that are not very useful without the other half of the correspondence, there are trivia such as automobile repair receipts and newspaper clippings, mostly about heavy water, a popular subject not only for news but also humor.

An extremely valuable source of information, especially about the early days at Berkeley and about his colleagues has been the book "From Retorts to Lasers:

The Story of Chemistry at Berkeley" by Prof. William L. Jolly [201]. Professor Jolly did not overlap with Lewis, but came to the department only a few years later in 1949 when memories were still sharp. He has well described the history from the beginning of the department and the college up to the mid 1980's.

A publication "In Honor of Gilbert Newton Lewis" [202] put out by the University on the occasion of his seventieth birthday has been very useful for it consists of a brief list of honors, an anonymous tribute and a list of all his publications up to that date and a list of all department PhDs from 1913 to 1945.

These sources have been extensively supplemented by the various obituaries, especially one written by Joel Hildebrand[203], a colleague at Berkeley for all but one year of Lewis's Berkeley career and also was familiar with the military period. The published scientific papers have been the main source for the technical basis of this account.

A biographical book, "Borderland of the Unknown" by Arthur Lachman [204] has been very useful, especially for more personal recollections.

Finally, I must give credit to Mr. Harold Paretchan for his untiring and extraordinary efforts to document G. N. Lewis' eminent position among chemists and scientists of his period. Mr. Paretchan, a resident of Weymouth, MA, started on this search in 1993 having been prompted by his discovery that Lewis was born in Weymouth but no one in that city knew this fact, nor had any idea who Lewis had been. Although Paretchan is not a chemist, a very cursory investigation made it clear that he had come upon a man of great distinction, worthy of further search. Harold Paretchan has found records at Harvard and at MIT telling much about the early career of his subject, and has unstintingly shared these with me. Much of the drive for writing this biography has come from him.

The part of this biography based on my memory is thin until the middle thirties when I was old enough to know what was going on and close enough to begin to appreciate the chemistry. I was an undergraduate at Berkeley from 1935 to 1940 and saw a great deal of my father since I lived at home, although I saw little of him at the University. In 1940 I went away to graduate school, and saw him much less, but I was able to understand more of what he was doing in the brief periods that I was at home during summers. From 1944 to the summer of 1946 I was in the Navy. I was in electronic technician's schools in California from the winter of 1944 to the winter of 1945, even for a period on neighboring Treasure Island. In this period I saw him frequently and was told especially about the Ice Age[166] and the Civilization in America[167] papers which by that time were occupying much of

4

his attention. He died while I was in New York in the Navy. After his death and after my discharge from the Navy near Berkeley I returned to Harvard in the fall of 1946 to finish my PhD in 1947. Thus my memory is that of a child for the early period with increasingly close personal and scientific contact until three months before his unexpected death.

This biography was started about eight years after my mother's death in 1987 and so this source of information was closed to me. I keep thinking of things that I should have asked her. My brother, who died in 1992, would also have been a major source, if I had started earlier.

Several of my father's colleagues at Berkeley could have been very helpful had they been alive. I regret that I had no discussions with either Melvin Calvin or Kenneth Pitzer, both of whom died very recently well after the start of writing this biography. This was to some extent ameliorated since both contributed to the Las Vegas meeting.

The personal part is enriched by some of my sister Margery Selby's memories going back a few years farther than mine. She is not a chemist, but as a family member her comments have been extremely useful. She has also supplied me with a bound collection of reprints covering all the Lewis work up through 1916. Margery has read early drafts and made many suggestions throughout. Her daughter, Sylvia, who knew him as "Grandy" in the first years of her life, contributed some memories. Sylvia (Alcon) has also offered valuable suggestions on organization and style.

A number of memorabilia of our family were in the possession of my brother Richard. He had these in Inverness, California, our childhood home, where he had retired after a career mostly in the chemical industry. These were dispersed on his death and that of his wife Helen only a few months later, partly to his four children. They have been helpful to me in trying to put things together.

Chapter I. Lewis's Life and Career up to 1912

Gilbert Newton Lewis was born in Weymouth, MA on Oct 23, 1875. The second child and first son of Francis (Frank) Wesley and Mary Burr White Lewis. The early childhood years in Weymouth have left no record, except that the location of the house is known and there is a 1880 census record.

His ancestry is fairly clear on the Lewis side; it has been traced by his son Richard in his contribution[205] "A Pioneer Spirit from a Pioneer Family" to the Las Vegas Symposium. An abridged version is here presented. His ancestry goes back to the first Lewis in America, George Lewis, who came to Massachusetts from Kent in England in 1632, and was one of the founders of the town of Barnstable. A fire in Barnstable destroyed many of the records, but there are later many Lewises in the town. One of these, Jabez Lewis, moved with his family and a few other families in the early 1790s to a virtual wilderness in what is now West Claremont, New Hampshire, and Gilbert Lewis's grandfather was Jabez's grandson, George Gilbert Lewis. George Gilbert and his wife Adeline Labaree Lewis (who was descended from a French trapper, Pierre Labaree) had five sons including Frank Lewis, Gilbert's father, and at least one daughter. All five sons graduated from Dartmouth College. Frank became a lawyer in Weymouth, MA, and married Mary Burr White of Massachusetts.

Frank Lewis was clearly a capable and intelligent man. He was a lawyer and later a banker. He wrote a book "State Insurance" published in 1909 which was said to anticipate ideas later to appear as Social Security; it is not known whether President F. D. Roosevelt or his advisers had ever seen this book before establishing the Social Security system in the 1930s. Gilbert's mother, née Mary Burr White, participated extensively in his education. Her antecedents are not as well traced. Her father, Newton White, was described by Gilbert's sister Mary (our Aunt Polly) as a "Great and good man" according to my brother [205].

According to the 1850 census[206] Newton White lived in the Randolph township in Norwalk county, MA. He was 36 at the time and is listed as a farmer. He had four daughters, of whom Mary Burr White was the third. His property was valued at $2000, neither very small or large for the time and place. The suggestion that the middle name may have come from Aaron Burr is a possible connection to someone of great intellect and notoriety. However, Aaron Burr, Jr. himself (at one time vice president of the United States) had no legitimate descendants except a daughter who in turn had only a son who died young and without issue.

There were a number of other Burrs in New England at the time, and the source of my grandmother's name has not been traced. In terms of ancestry we see no conspicuous signs of unusual intellectual distinction although most of the family appears to have been of good ability and education. Incidentally, the suggestion that Gilbert Newton Lewis was named presciently after the much earlier eminent scientists William Gilbert and Isaac Newton is clearly wrong; he was named after his two grandfathers.

An interesting story showing how short our history really is was told me by my father. When he was a small boy, he shook hands with a man who had shaken hands with George Washington. I calculate that if my father was five at this encounter and this man was himself five when he met Washington just before his death in 1799, then he would have had to be 86 or more when my father met him. It would have been quite possible.

Frank and Mary's son, Gilbert Newton Lewis, had an older sister, Mary (Aunt Polly), born in 1871 and a younger brother, Roger Labaree Lewis, born in 1884. I never met Frank but did briefly know my grandmother Mary Burr White Lewis, when she was over 80 and lived with us in California before she died. It was then hard to see her as the major tutor of my father since she was by that time very forgetful and senile. My sister Margery remembers better than I do a single visit from Uncle Roger in Inverness, a town about forty miles north of San Franciso where we had a summer and sometime year-round house. She was favorably impressed by Uncle Roger, who was in the movie industry in Hollywood for the latter part of his life. Once I saw his name in the list of credits for a movie.

We saw more of Aunt Polly, who came out to California more than once that I remember. This contact continued up to my graduate student days, when she asked me to spend Christmas (1942?) with her in Cleveland. She had by that time retired, but was living comfortably. I remember it better because it was my only white Christmas ever in spite of several winters in graduate school in Cambridge. I remember my first attempt to drive barely adequately on snowy streets in Cleveland in my aunt's car and the vivid color of a cardinal against the snow in her back yard. Unfortunately, I remember nothing of conversations about the family. This characteristic of mine of remembering objects much better than people and their conversations makes writing this biography especially difficult for me.

We can look for factors that contributed to my father's distinction. Four possibilities stand out. First is his ancestry, second is his education, which was unusual, third he had few distractions, and finally he started his professional careerat a time that thermodynamics was ripe for exploitation.

A very uncommon education certainly contributed to Gilbert's later distinction. His early education was far from conventional then and would be even more so now. He did not go to elementary school at all, nor to very much high school. He was taught at home to learn reading (complete by the age of five, and he could read a great deal even at three). There is no doubt that he was educated to a level far beyond anyone of his age in the public schools. Lewis was not alone in learning reading while very young. Extraordinary precocity appears among several chemists mentioned in this biography. Thus Svante Arrhenius was also reported to be able to read at a very early age[207]. Theodore William Richards was also precocious and entered Haverford college at the age of fourteen[208].

Although there is no record of it, it is possible that some of the burden of teaching Gilbert and his sister and brother may possibly have been fallen on his aunt Miriam Lewis, who later taught school in Salt Lake City. Somewhere along the way Lewis learned French and German, arithmetic, algebra, and at least some Latin, Greek and history. His German was quite adequate for reading and understanding the spoken language, but Lachman[204] commented that his pronunciation was incredibly awful. In his postdoctoral year in Germany he must have been able to make himself understood in German, for the universality of English as the language of science was a long way off. I recall no evidence of his Latin or Greek skills, except that some knowledge of Latin (and possibly Greek) was then and for many years later a requirement for the AB degree from Harvard.

The 1880 census in Weymouth [209] listed the family as his mother and father, him, his sister, Mary, and his aunt Miriam Lewis. He moved in 1884 with his family to near Lincoln, Nebraska when he was nine and the home schooling continued for several more years. The exact date of this move is obscure; his brother Roger was born in that year. His father, Frank Lewis, joined a business called "Western Investments." I do not know if he practiced law there or if he was even a member of the bar. Gilbert Lewis continued his home education, then went to the University of Nebraska School (apparently a sort of prep. school) in 1888 and later to the University of Nebraska for about three years.

This early education was shared with his older sister, Mary (Aunt Polly). She later founded her own private school in Cleveland to teach children the way she thought it should be done. The school and her policies were controversial, I only heard hints of a possibly scandalous situation, and I met her for the first extended time when she invited me for Christmas in Cleveland, well after she had retired. She certainly was not a simple schoolteacher and she may well have had Gilbert's intellect and nonconforming ideas. It is not established whether Uncle Roger was subject to the same education as his two siblings, but he graduated from Harvard in the class of '06, only a year older than his brother Gilbert at graduation.

The attempt to attribute the G. N. Lewis genius to his education is partly successful, but although it is unusual it is not unique, there must be thousands of Americans of his generation who had similar backgrounds. Almost universal school attendance is a rather recent development and in a place where good schools were hard to find a substantial number of children must have learned a great deal at home, if they had educated parents. We can look to see if there were other factors contributing.

There is much emphasis now on athletics in schools and colleges. The strong, tall athlete is in demand, but he must be extraordinarily talented to do well at academic subjects. Indeed, at most institutions the "Scholar-Athlete" is a prized and unfortunately rare student. The academic advantage of a student so small in stature that he is effectively ineligible for football or basketball must be perceptible. The popular image is the "nerd," who is represented as small, badly coordinated, and usually with thick glasses. G. N. Lewis was about 5'7", he was in his youth slight but neither badly coordinated nor nearsighted. I suggest that such a stature impaired student may have a small but perceptible educational advantage; such a student would be able to devote full time to academic work. At most this could have been a minor contributor to Lewis's distinction. The lack of distractions continued for many years, for he postponed marriage to the age of 36.

Lewis certainly came along at an opportune time in the development of physical chemistry. Chemical thermodynamics had been started only a few years earlier; it was based on a number of approximations and was therefore not rigorous. Lewis was able to recognize and eliminate the approximations and to devise a new system that added rigor, yet was at the same time practical and useful. He clearly started his work at the right time.

We can thus see that the factors referred to above, ancestry, education, lack of distractions, and timing may have helped Lewis to develop into the extraordinary man that he became. However, these factors are clearly insufficient to explain his exceptional talents.

The travels over the generations from England to Massachusetts to New Hampshire, back to Massachusetts, to Nebraska, to Harvard, to Germany, to the Phillipine Islands, back to Massachusetts again, and finally to California suggested the term pioneer family to my brother Dick and the description of G. N. Lewis as a pioneer spirit who himself undertook travel to the last six locations[205]. The pioneering nature of his science is better described elsewhere.

The family moved to Nebraska in 1884. They lived in the country close to Lincoln on what he referred to as a farm. He learned to appreciate delights of nature and had a favorite cow. He mentioned the sounds of the birds in the uncommon trees (Nebraska was called "The Tree Planting State" before it was the "Corn Husker State"). He spoke to us of the winter snow and ice; he described skating on ice encrusting the snow after a thaw.

The motives for moving to Nebraska become clearer when one realizes that the times from 1880 to 1890 were boom years there. Lincoln doubled in population from 1885 to 1887 and the rest of the state also more than doubled its population from 1880 (pop. 0.43 million) to 1890 (pop. more than 1 million). It is understandable how a man like Frank Lewis would want to participate in this boom, and how he could leave with his family as soon as the boom was over and return to the more stable Boston environment. The move to the near frontier at Nebraska is consistent with the description of the Lewis family as pioneers. Indeed the boom collapsed in the early 1890s; the population of the state stabilized to something over a million at this time, and is now (1990) only about 1.6 million. Of course Gilbert would have been rather insensitive to these economic fluctuations.

His home education has been described above, it continued during his early years in Nebraska. He went to the University of Nebraska School in 1888 and then the University of Nebraska, where he completed three years. My sister Margery remembers his description of walking for miles to school through the snow. However, this story sounds like the traditional story told to children who resent having to walk to school; it may be an exaggeration.

He transferred to Harvard in 1893, graduating with the class of 1896. Apparently he did well at Harvard, but he is said to have failed a course in organic chemistry. Most of the brief histories suggest that this transfer was due to his disappointment in the Nebraska education. However, he was only 17 and his father, Frank Lewis, left Lincoln at the same time for reasons described above to become an executive of the Merchants Trust Company in Boston. Presumably the whole family moved with him, with the possible exception of Gilbert's aunt Miriam (who at some date moved to Salt Lake City where she taught school and lived the rest of her life). Thus the motive for moving to Harvard may have been merely to keep the family together with their father, or it may have been that Frank moved back to Boston in order to give his talented son, Gilbert, a better educational opportunity, or both. Gilbert's comments about the value of his Nebraska formal training were far from favorable; he felt that he would have graduated from Harvard earlier if he had not lost a great deal of credit in transferring from the University of Nebraska.

After graduating from Harvard he taught for one year at Phillips Andover academy, an exclusive prep. school, where he is quoted in a Harvard class of 1896 publication[210] as teaching whatever no one else wanted to teach, and developing lasting bad golf habits.

He returned to Harvard for graduate work under T. W. Richards, receiving the AM in 1898 and the PhD in 1899. The PhD thesis was on "Some Electro-chemical and Thermochemical Relations of Zinc and Cadmium Amalgams"; it was published as his first paper[1] and the only one formally jointly with Richards. He also published[2] at that time "The Development and Application of a General Equation for Free Energy and Physico-chemical Equilibrium". There is some uncertainty about the MA thesis; it has been lost, but there has been a suggestion that it contained some of his atomic structure ideas. I am inclined to doubt that suggestion since he would have referred to it later instead of to the drawings of cubes from an old notebook for an undergraduate lecture that he reproduced in the "Valence and the Structure of Atoms and Molecules" book[78]. He stayed on for one year as instructor in chemistry, then went on leave to Germany. It is worth a digression to recall that physical chemistry had not been a recognized field for very long. A contribution[211] to the Lewis symposium by J. W. Servos: "G. N. Lewis: The Disciplinary Setting" describes how recent were ideas such as ionization in solution proposed by Arrhenius, the dilution law of Ostwald; even the existence of atoms and molecules was debated. The newest physical chemistry was brought to Harvard by T. W. Richards, who had returned from Ostwald's laboratory only the year before Lewis took a course with him.

Servos quotes a 1922 letter from Lewis to E. C. Bingham saying: 'The fact is that physical chemistry no longer exists....Physical chemists have developed a large number of useful methods by which the concrete problems of inorganic chemistry, organic chemistry, biochemistry, and technical chemistry may be attacked, and as these methods grow more numerous, it becomes increasingly difficult to adhere to our older classification". This seems at variance with Lewis' later comment that "physical chemistry is anything interesting". (I have heard this quotation so often that I cannot trace its origin).

Servos describes the high level of experimental skill fostered by Richards, but points out Richards' caution about the use of imagination in constructing hypotheses not firmly based on experiment. Lewis had already embarked on a career of imaginative and creative ideas, some of which were wrong, but many were correct, and these stimulated still newer concepts; all these contributed to his reputation.

Richards had been dead for years by the time I came to Harvard, but his widow was still in good health although quite elderly. On hearing that I played the violin, she asked me to come to her house to play violin-piano sonatas. She was still an accomplished pianist. We played one of the Brahms sonatas, and she told me that as a young girl she had looked forward to the publication of a new Brahms sonata. I mention this because we now feel that Brahms, who died in 1897, belongs way back in the almost forgotten past.

Lewis spent the year 1900 to 1901 in Germany with Ostwald in Leipzig and with Nernst in Göttingen, these were the outstanding physical chemists of that time. The association with at least one of them was almost obligatory for an American physical chemist in research. There seem to be no publications coming from this German period. While in Germany he "learned the pleasures of shocking the chemical establishment with his novel ideas, a taste he retained through his life." Ostwald[211] wrote "All in all I think Dr. Lewis is a competent and learned man." I do not find any record of Nernst's opinion of Lewis, but some relevant suggestions are to be found in the chapter "The Nobel Prize?"

He returned to Harvard as instructor and stayed until 1904 This was a scientifically unproductive period; there is one published paper in 1901 and the next paper comes from Manila. His later comments were that there was no interest in or discussion of new ideas among the Harvard chemistry faculty. The picture of cubical atoms apparently arose from this period, for the pictures from the 1916 paper[55] and sketches reproduced in the book[78] "Valence and the Structure of Atoms and Molecules" are from a notebook of 1902 connected with an undergraduate course. A later letter to R. A. Millikan, in 1919, quoted in Jolly's book[201], says ".... I had much the same ideas of atomic and molecular structure as I now hold, and I had a much greater desire to expound them, but I could not find a soul sufficiently interested to hear the theory." It will be noted that this letter was written well after the 1916 paper[55] on "The Atom and the Molecule". Later, in Berkeley, he was known to discuss almost every paper with colleagues before publication, so deprivation of such interactions was for him almost devastating.

Lewis was a member of the "Wicht" club[212]. As far as I can tell, this was an organization of a few like-minded academic men. It started among a group at Harvard but may have continued for years. In his words[212] "These years at

Harvard, and indeed all subsequent years, were made richer by the organization of a group of eleven men, then engaged in academic pursuits at Harvard, under the name of the Wicht Club. This remarkable organization, in which were discussed with the utmost candor all the problems of science and of society, left a profound impression upon the minds and characters of all of its members."

My awareness of this club was based only on two images, in the first we had a painting of a weird creature in the woods with a conical shape called a Wicht with one clawed foot (like that of a bird) showing underneath a red cloak covering everything with only two eyes showing. When we would ask what it was a picture of, he would tell us that it was a Wicht. Another similar illustration of this Wicht appeared on a beer mug. In my father's office there were a few volumes of a work with the title on the spine "Was wichtiges" (What is important?), which unfortunately I never saw opened. I later surmised that the title of these volumes is related to the name of the club and its mascot. This club may have continued on to the Berkeley days, I have very little information about it. However my mother recalled a time when my father went to a costume party as a Wicht; a pair of shoes became unusable because one of them was converted to the single claw of the Wicht. My attempt to reconstruct the membership has been unfruitful; two names come up as possibilities, Walter Cannon and Harry Morse; they were both old friends of Lewis and both were at Harvard between 1896 and 1905.

In 1904, Lewis accepted a position as superintendent of weights and measures in Manila, in the Phillipine Islands. There have been many guesses as to why he took a position in such a remote place. Some suggest that it was to get away from what he regarded as the stifling atmosphere of Harvard. In his symposium talk[205], my brother Richard called him a pioneer, and going to the Phillipines certainly fits this description. The thermodynamic research continued in what he described, perhaps not entirely seriously, as a splendid government laboratory. Later, he says that this laboratory, the Bureau of Science, was recently demolished[212]. He completed a study of the thermal dissociation of silver oxide using minimal equipment. Although he enjoyed this exotic experience, it still lacked stimulation from colleagues. It seems likely that he formulated a good deal in his mind during this time, for a gush of papers with no coauthors appeared as soon as he came back from this tropical position.

When he came back he had renewed enthusiasm for research as well as an addiction to Philippine cigars. These were in the early days "Fighting Bobs" that came in a long box with the inscription "Regular 10¢ value, now 5¢." These were made of Phillipine mahogany, not in that location a rare or expensive wood.

(The name was a tribute to Admiral Robley D. Evans, possibly a participant in the battle of Manila bay in 1898. This is worth mentioning because major hostilities derived from the Spanish-American war had stopped only three years before Lewis went to Manila) The switch to "Alhambra" cigars (in a more nearly square box) came much later in the thirties when the total US market for the Fighting Bob brand shrank to a single customer. It was one of these Alhambra boxes that Glenn Seaborg has displayed as the first container for plutonium. Lewis was always generous with his Phillipine cigars, but found few takers. The level of this habit was between twelve and twenty a day, usually about seventeen. During the World War II when Phillipine cigars of any brand became unavailable, he tried all sorts of alternatives; he smoked a briar pipe, corncob pipes, but seldom cigarettes as far as I know, he tried Havana cigars, but he claimed that these were much too strong for his taste. He also claimed that he did not inhale the smoke.

He returned to Massachusetts to accept a position at MIT (then in Boston) which he held from 1905 to 1912 as a member of the Research Laboratory of Physical Chemistry. This was an enormously talented group assembled by A. A. Noyes starting in 1903. Lewis rose through the ranks to the title of professor, and was making a name for himself as an already distinguished physical chemist. It was a very productive time, both in experimental work and in theory. A series papers on electrode potentials and a number of other equilibrium measurements constituted a major contribution to the thermodynamic work which occupied much of his talent for over twenty years. His work was firmly based on the theoretical treatment of J. Willard Gibbs, which had been widely ignored by the chemists of the day. A story about a meeting between Lewis and Gibbs is presented later.

During the latter years of this period, while still continuing his thermodynamic research, he also served as administrator of this group for several years starting before his promotion to professor because Noyes had been given a higher administrative position. This administrative experience undoubtedly impressed President Wheeler and Dean O'Neill as an important factor, along with his outstanding research, in making the decision to offer Lewis the combined professorship and the position of dean of the College of Chemistry at Berkeley. In this MIT period he also became an advocate of Einstein's special relativity, and described presenting a lecture to a hostile group of physicists on this subject; he published several papers with his MIT colleagues on this subject in spite of the hostility. It turned out not to be the last time that he opposed the conventional views of physicists.

This very productive period in his career ended when Lewis decided to accept a position at the University of California in Berkeley.

Chapter II. Publications through 1912

Lewis' reputation is to a large extent based on his publications; there are about 168 of these. These appear in about 25 different journals, but mostly in the *Journal of the American Chemical Society* (97), *Physical Review* (17), *Proceedings of the National Academy of Sciences* (16), *Zeitschrift für physikalische Chemie* (13) (most, but not all, of these were German versions of English language papers), and *Proceedings of the American Academy* (11). This dual publication in German was rather customary at this time, the abandonment of this custom might possibly be due to the increasing reputation of American chemistry. In Lewis' case, adherence to this custom stopped about 1910.

He did not like speaking in public, he presented very little of his work at scientific meetings and relied heavily on the written word to carry his message. He was, however, a master of the written word and numerous examples are widely quoted to show this. I shall therefore show here a summary of the published work before 1912, in rough chronological order, but with little scientific detail. His thesis and only three other papers (on thermodynamics) preceded his escape to Manila. Three papers[5, 6, 7] published from his time in Manila, are of course a tribute to his insatiable appetite for research. His use of the simplest apparatus to measure oxygen pressure over silver oxide typified to an extreme his long-lasting preference for simple apparatus, characteristic of nearly all his work up to the end.

Once back in Massachusetts at MIT his productivity increased. An early paper from the MIT time was "Outlines of a New System of Thermodynamic Chemistry"[17] which laid the groundwork for much of the thermodynamic work leading eventually to the publication of the book by Lewis and Randall in 1923[77]. In this important 1907 paper, he described how the imprecise use of pressures and concentrations could be made exact by using fugacity and activity respectively, thus avoiding assumptions about ideality of gases or solutions. It allowed an element of rigor in chemical thermodynamics which had previously been lacking. Although this was not his first presentation of these ideas, it was the most complete and is now the most readable, in part because the notation was much the same as that used later in Lewis and Randall. In this time at MIT he published almost forty papers.

The publications from his MIT period were mostly on thermodynamics, many were those anticipated by the 1907 paper mentioned above, but they also included his first paper on color[11], and one on relativity with R. C. Tolman[24], followed by others on this subject, and one on four dimensional vector analysis[29].

A prime example of the experimental work he was involved with was the classic 1910 paper with C. A. Kraus[30] on the sodium electrode, one of several showing the electrochemical approach to thermodynamics. In this paper the problem of the reactivity of sodium with water was attacked by comparing an intermediate dilute sodium amalgam electrode which was not reactive with water to the reference electrode, then comparing it with a pure sodium electrode in an inert nonaqueous (amine) solvent. He was quite proud of this work and told me once that this study would have been impossible without the marvelous experimental skill of Kraus. This was the forerunner of later papers on the potassium[34], lithium[41] and rubidium[52] electrodes, the last done at Berkeley, with one of his first graduate students there, William Argo.

Lewis was one of the early believers in Einstein's special relativity. The oft reported meeting between Lewis and Einstein is now documented[213], the letter reproduced below seems at best to refer to a very brief contact.

The following letter was sent to Einstein in Berlin on February 23, 1921:

"My dear Professor Einstein:

Many things have happened since the very pleasant Kneipe that I had with you and Bredig in Zurich. Not the least of these is the wide-spread acceptance and appreciation of your theories, which has delighted me and for which I offer you my sincere congratulations.

I learn by this morning's paper that you are going to be in this country in the near future. I hope that on this occasion you will find it possible to visit California. It is a wonderful country, and I am sure that if your time permits you would find the trip across the continent of much interest.

If you could arrange to come it would be a great pleasure to me to offer you such hospitality as our home affords, and I could arrange with the University to pay your traveling expenses from the Atlantic coast, without any obligations on your part, such as formal lectures. It need be nothing more than a pleasure trip.

With cordial regards, I am,

Yours very sincerely,"(No signature appears on the carbon copy)

Einstein's reply is not dated; a reply on Zionist Organization of America stationary from New York declines this offer due to the press of time in connection with a mission to promote the proposed University of Jerusalem, but acknowledges the previous encounter with the sentence: "It would be a great pleasure for me to meet you again and also to see your very interesting country". It should be noted that a round trip by train to California would take at best well over a week. As far as I can translate the word "Kneipe" it appears to mean that they met for a beer. A copy of this letter from Einstein is in the photograph section.

Lewis published papers[20,24,25] on relativity well before this new physics was generally accepted. He told me much later that his mathematical background was rather minimal, and that he regretted not having studied it earlier. E. B. Wilson noted, as quoted by Lachman[204]: "Lewis had a very original mind - he was a fine theoretical physicist and chemist - he was not an accomplished mathematician technically but a sort of natural mathematician....." He had an excellent qualitative understanding of special relativity, as shown much later in the Silliman lecture book[93], "The Anatomy of Science", published in 1926. He managed to find coworkers of great mathematical talent, for example Richard Tolman and E. B. Wilson, when faced with more difficult mathematics. Most of the rest of his published papers after 1913 were from Berkeley.

Chapter III: The Berkeley and California Environment.

California was a remote and inaccessible place until the discovery of gold, which led to the '49 gold rush and shortly after to statehood. California was accessible from the east coast only by a difficult and stormy trip around the Horn or by long wagon train trip across the great desert. In fact access from Asia by sea was the most practical, partly accounting for the large number of Chinese laborers building the railway. The establishment of large Asian communities on the west coast originated with these workers. The transcontinental railway was completed in 1869, and the wagon trains became instantly obsolete. The opening of the Panama canal in 1914 greatly shortened the sea access from the east coast to California. This opening was celebrated by the opening of the Panama-Pacific International exposition in San Francisco, and a few traces of this exposition still remain. This was the setting for the arrival of Lewis and his new faculty to Berkeley.

In 1910, Berkeley had a population of about 40,000, a number about three times that from the previous census in 1900 compared to today's population of well over 100,000, and it was a very different city, much more self-contained than it is now. It was connected to San Francisco by a ferry system with electric train service or street cars to the ferry terminals at each end. There were street cars for local surface transportation which extended into Oakland, but Berkeley had within the city limits shops and department stores that do not exist today mostly concentrated on Shattuck avenue and around the Sather Gate entrance to the campus. It was a safe city; even more than twenty years later when I was at school and the university, I walked everywhere without any concerns, as did everyone else. Then, as now, the university was a major contributor to the city.

Across the bay, San Francisco was recovering from the 1906 fire and earthquake, but was still ten times as big as Berkeley. It was not yet a placid city; the infamous Barbary Coast with its sinister reputation of shanghaiing sailors as well as a center for most of the more lurid sins had only partly faded away after surviving intact up to the fire.[214] The change for Lewis and his colleagues from highly civilized Boston was drastic; much of California was only decades away from complete lawlessness. Berkeley, doubtless due to its location on a shallow part of the bay and therefore not suitable for ships to dock, did not have the rowdy spirit of the seaport of San Francisco, and was even then a pleasant residential city.

The University of California was established in 1868 just before the opening of the railway; it occupied a location in downtown Oakland before moving in about five years to its present site in Berkeley. A chemistry building was opened in 1890, it lasted for nearly three quarters of a century. Berkeley and the university were spared major damage from the earthquake and the much more destructive fire across the bay. As a consequence the first building on the campus, South Hall, is still (as of 1997) in use.

The State of California was not a scientific or educational center in the early days. The University of California was joined by the University of Southern California in 1880 and by Stanford University in 1885, but other institutions came somewhat later. The Throop Institute started in 1891 as a technical high school and grew slowly to become the very strong California Institute of Technology, but did not get this name until 1920, UCLA did not become a full university campus until 1919, and the agricultural school of the University at Davis dates from 1906.

The Berkeley chemistry department was small and undistinguished for the most part; an exception was Frederick Cottrell, the inventor of the Cottrell precipitator for reducing particulate emissions from stacks. This device was very profitable and the proceeds were used to fund the Research Corporation, which then and now continues to provide research money to mostly junior science faculty members throughout the country (including me when I was an assistant professor at Rice). It was in fact the resignation of Cottrell from the department that led to the need for another professor and to the recruitment of G. N. Lewis in 1912.

The subsequent American participation in the First World War brought Berkeley and the University closer to the rest of the country. The San Francisco Bay area was involved in ship building as a part of the war effort. A little more than a decade after the war came the great depression, starting in the crash of 1929; it included a period of severe labor unrest especially among the San Francisco longshoremen. This culminated in violence and in continued strikes lasting for years. The result of this was that shipping almost abandoned the port of San Francisco, and the port has not been as important since. I remember crossing to San Francisco sometime in the mid 1930's seeing many ships at anchor in the bay, idled by the long strike.

The late thirties saw the construction of bridges connecting the cities around the bay. The Golden Gate Bridge for automobile traffic was first, then the San Francisco-Oakland Bay Bridge which then bore both automobile traffic and electric trains came next. Finally the Richmond-San Rafael Bridge completed a circle of modern automobile bridges around the bay. The system of ferries was then dismantled, (although one passenger ferry, across the Golden Gate, was started again many years later) to the regret of those who appreciated the pause in the traffic worries while on the ferry. However, the automobile trip to either San

Francisco or Inverness became much faster. The electric train system, called BART, going through a tunnel under the bay to connect San Francisco to the East Bay came much later.

Chapter IV. Career, 1912 to 1946

In 1912 Lewis had a reputation as a stellar physical chemist of the first magnitude. He came to the attention of the Department of Chemistry of the University of California and the president, Benjamin Ide Wheeler. At their invitation he visited the campus and, on being offered the position of Professor, Chairman of the Department, and Dean of the College of Chemistry, he returned to MIT and then sent a list of conditions for accepting the offer. These included a carefully itemized 50% increase in the salary budget, immediate construction of a temporary building and immediate plans for a permanent building. The existing chemistry building had been built in 1890, it was deemed adequate but too small for the anticipated department size; it survived until 1963. There were also demands for apparatus and machine shop budget increases. These extensive demands, well documented in Jolly's book[201], were met and Lewis accepted. Three of his MIT colleagues were persuaded to join him: William Bray and Richard Tolman, with Merle Randall as his private assistant. These men constituted the new nucleus of the department for many years.

A Harvard Alumni publication made the following note at about this time: "'96- G. N. Lewis, now Research Professor of Chemistry in the Massachusetts Institute of Technology, has been elected Professor of Chemistry in the University of California. He will take with him to California several members of the staff of the Institute, and it is the purpose that he shall considerably develop the department of chemistry at California". It will be seen that considerable development was a serious understatement.

It must have taken an adventurous spirit for Lewis, as professor and dean, Bray and Tolman as assistant professors and Randall as a private assistant to Lewis, and then Gibson and Hildebrand a year later to come from secure positions to start on a new career at this remote outpost. For Lewis, it was an extension of the pioneer spirit[205] that he perhaps inherited from the ancestor who left England for the New World, the more recent ancestor who left Massachusetts for the frontier in New Hampshire, and his father who left New England to make his fortune in Nebraska. Nevertheless, as it has been for a century, it was a good living environment and it very soon became a fabulously good scientific environment, so it was fairly easy to convince a student to come to Berkeley for graduate work. After the recruitment of Gibson and Hildebrand it was unnecessary to convince faculty to come because for the next twenty years the senior faculty was all home grown, and few who had tenure left for other positions. The faculty in 1912 was composed of Biddle, Blasdale, Booth, Morgan and O'Neill from the earlier period, and Lewis, Bray, and Tolman, with Randall as a research assistant to Lewis (later with a faculty appointment) as the new additions. Gibson and Hildebrand were recruited to the faculty in 1913. Additions in the next more than twenty years were entirely Berkeley PhDs.

In an illustrated article[215] "The College of Chemistry in the G. N. Lewis era: 1912-1946", Melvin Calvin and Glenn Seaborg describe the development of the department. Between them they knew every permanent member of the faculty in that period except O'Neill, Booth, and Biddle. They included several photographs, one taken in front of the temporary building that Lewis had demanded in accepting the professorship and deanship, showing some of the faculty, staff and students. This building was later called the "Rat House", reflecting a short time use by biologically oriented faculty and students. I remember it in my time as being mostly Rollefson's domain. Another picture was taken on the front steps of Gilman Hall shortly after it opened in 1917; it was built instead of the requested addition to the older chemistry building. It shows nearly all the faculty and staff. All the pictures show as an essential part of the department William Cummings, the glass blower.

Lewis is recognizable in all the pictures as the shortest one with the beard, which he kept till after the first war. To emphasize his stature, he appears in these pictures next to his very tall student and later colleague, William Argo. The final picture was taken in front of the new building Gilman Hall in 1920. It shows the department, including George Nelson, machinist, (inventor of the Nelson pump, a rotary oil pump widely used in the department). He, along with Cummings, were still around through my time as an undergraduate. Lewis is now shown without the beard, but still with the mustache which he kept till the end, except for a short time when the drama section of the University required a different appearance. The three photographs together show all the members of Lewis' department except E. Booth, who died in 1917, H. C. Biddle, who resigned from the department in 1918, and W. C. Morgan, who resigned in 1912 to take a position at Reed College. However, Glenn Seaborg did know Morgan when he later became a member of the UCLA faculty well before Seaborg was an undergraduate there.

Lewis' career as professor and dean was interrupted in 1918 by the First World War. In December, 1917, Lewis was commissioned a major in what became the Chemical Warfare Service in the army. I do not know the details of this new position, that is whether he volunteered, or whether he was convinced that he was needed by the Chemical Warfare Service. He left very soon after for France, where he was made Director of the Chemical Warfare Service laboratory and shortly afterward Chief of the Defense Division of the Chemical Warfare Service. He spent a short time at the front, mostly for the experience, but also to help him realize the magnitude of the problem of gas defense. When he returned from the front he established the Gas Defense School whose graduates had a marked effect in reducing gas casualties from a major hazard to a rather small one by mid 1918. He left for Washington just before the armistice, and was promoted to the rank of Lieutenant Colonel and was made Chief of the Training Division of the Chemical Warfare Service. For his effective service and training programs he was made Chevalier of the French Legion of Honor and was later given the US Distinguished Service Medal. The source I have used for this army experience is the extended obituary by Hildebrand[203]. Hildebrand was especially qualified to write on Lewis' wartime service, for he was also in the Chemical Warfare Service at the same time, and received the Distinguished Service Medal in a joint ceremony with Lewis in 1922. For this short wartime period, E. C. O'Neill served as dean and department chairman.

One story, which I heard many times, that Lewis brought back was about a controversy about the toxicity of hydrogen cyanide or prussic acid. There was a suggestion from the French authorities that this would make an effective war gas since it is quite toxic, very volatile, and inexpensive. Tests had shown that it would kill dogs very rapidly. Contrarily, British authorities claimed that dogs were especially sensitive, and hence data based on these tests were inconclusive. A British gas officer settled the matter by going into the gas chamber with a dog (probably French), the gas was turned on, and shortly the Briton emerged from the chamber with the dead dog. Lewis is quoted[204] as saying that this was one of the most striking examples of devotion to duty that he had ever come across. Much later the state of California used for many years the gas chamber with hydrogen cyanide as the legal method of capital punishment, so clearly the French were not very far from being correct. I recall a photograph of my father in uniform from this period, wearing a pointed black beard that made him look very severe.

After returning from the war, Lewis spent the rest of his career in Berkeley. Only occasional professional trips, one sabbatical leave, taken mostly at Oxford University in 1923 and a few family trips and vacations took him away from his work. In the early twenties he was busy writing "Thermodynamics" and "Valence", both published in 1923. "The Anatomy of Science" was published in 1926 after the Silliman lectures at Yale on which it is based. No further books were written, but half his papers were published from 1925 on. His time was spent after the first war with both research and administrative duties He remained active in his research work to the end of his life but university rules required that he retire from administrative duties in 1941, when he had passed the age of 65. It will be seen that his research remained not only active, but of very high quality in these semiretirement years.

Chapter V The Department

The development of the chemistry department at Berkeley is one of G. N. Lewis's greatest accomplishments. It can be described in terms of the students produced, in terms of accomplishments in teaching and research, in terms of the buildings, and the growth in numbers and distinction of his colleagues.

In 1912 before Lewis came there were not very many graduate students in chemistry. There are photographs[201] of freshman chemistry lectures showing two sections with about 100 students visible in each. After Lewis came the numbers in the freshman course were large; when I took the course in the middle thirties, the enrollment was over 1200, constituting nearly 10% of the university student body. The number who graduated with a degree in chemistry was of course much smaller.

There was thus a growth in the student population. The undergraduate growth is not well documented, the number of PhDs granted is clear [202]; there were two in 1914 and 16 in 1941. These PhDs were an excellent group, of the total in that period (244) 14 achieved tenure at Berkeley, five are Nobel laureates, many joined faculties at other major universities. A rough sampling of chemistry departments in some other universities showed that about one in six had a Berkeley background, in most cases the PhD.[216]

The Lewis research is documented elsewhere, but his colleagues were also creative in research.

A very few of the areas explored by his colleagues during the Lewis administration included the production of very low temperatures leading to more exact confirmation of the third law of thermodynamics, the exploration of inorganic reaction mechanisms, the study of photosynthesis using the newly discovered isotopes of carbon and oxygen, and the production of new isotopes of heavier elements. The study of solutions and the characterization of liquids was undertaken by more than one group, a study organic ligands of metal complexes not only was interesting in itself but turned out to be applicable to the later separation of transuranium elements as well as contributing to an oxygen producing process.

There were five faculty members when Lewis came in 1912, when he retired from administrative duties in 1941 there were 22. This growth in faculty is illustrated in the table below. Most of the data are derived from Jolly[201]. The table shows the inbred nature of the faculty; after the first two years only Calvin had a PhD from any other university. Randall had a degree from MIT; he came to Berkeley in 1912 but was not a faculty member until 1917.

University of California.   Chemistry Faculty 1912-1941

Name	PhD, Institution and director	Appointment date	Departure date
Booth, E,	(no PhD)	1878	1917 (d)
O'Neill, E. C.	Berk.	1879	1925 (ret)
Blasdale, W, C.	Berk.	1895	1941 (ret)
Biddle, H. C.	Chicago	1901	1918 (res)
Morgan, W. C.	Yale	1901	1913 (res)
Lewis, G. N.	Harvard, Richards	1912	1946 (d)
Bray, W. C.	Leipzig, Luther	1912	1946 (d)
Tolman, R. C.	MIT, Noyes	1912	1916 (res)
Gibson, G. E.	Breslau, Lummer	1913	1954 (ret)
Hildebrand, J.	Penn., Smith	1913	1954 (ret)
Branch, G.	Berk., Lewis	1915	1954 (d)
Randall, M.	MIT, Lewis	1917	1944(ret)
Eastman, E. D.	Berk., Lewis	1917	1945 (d)
Porter, C. W.	Berk., Biddle	1918	1946 (ret)
Stewart, T. D.	Berk., Tolman	1918	1957 (ret)
Latimer, W. M.	Berk., Gibson	1919	1955 (d)
Olson, A. R.	Berk., Lewis	1919	1954 (d)
Hogness, T. R.	Berk., Hildebrand	1921	1930 (res)
Giauque, W. F.	Berk., Gibson	1922	1982 (d)
Rollefson, G. K.	Berk., Lewis	1923	1955 (d)
Libby, W. F.	Berk., Latimer	1933	1942 (res)
Schutz, P. W.	Berk., Latimer	1933	1934 (res)
Pitzer, K. S.	Berk., Latimer	1937	1961 (res), reappointed '71 (d) 1997
Calvin, M.	Minnesota, Glockler	1937	1997 (d)
Seaborg, G. T.	Berk., Gibson	1939	-----------
Ruben, S.	Berk., Latimer and Libby	1939	1943 (d)

There were also about 40 shorter term appointments such as instructor. In 1941 there were three of these, J. W. Kennedy, J. J. Lingane and H. Taube.

In terms of physical facilities for research and teaching, three buildings were built. These included the "annex" or rathouse, laboratories for the freshman course, and a major building, Gilman Hall, where much of the research occurred.

Chapter VI: Publications and Research from 1913 on

After arrival in California and before the First World War, the Lewis publications are predominantly in thermodynamics. Thus, of 29 papers with publication dates between 1913 and 1918 inclusive, 23 are on electrode potentials or equilibria. One of these papers not on thermodynamics was the immensely influential one introducing the electron pair bond.[55] Some of the papers dated 1913 are from MIT; none later than this seem to be from MIT. Of these papers, approximately equal numbers were with graduate students and with faculty colleagues (counting Randall as faculty) and about 5 had no coauthors. This period ended when Lewis left for war service. The pioneering aspects of the thermodynamic work were the use of fugacities and activities on the one hand and later the treatment of solutions of electrolytes on the other.

The return to academic life after the war service was marked by no sudden change in his scientific output, indeed six papers published in 1918 and 1919 appear from their titles to be in the same vein as both earlier papers and later thermodynamic papers, yet they could not have been written by the method (described by some later coworkers) of dictation from Lewis to the coauthor, and indeed his contributions in this period must have been small in the late stages leading to publication. Two papers, without collaboration published in 1921 and 1922 are remote from the thermodynamic theme, the first on "Color and Chemical Constitution"[72] and the second on "The Chemistry of the Stars and the Evolution of Radioactive Substances"[75] represent further broadening of his interests beyond thermodynamics. Later papers and books will be sorted by subject.

In 1923 the book with Randall[77] "Thermodynamics and the Free Energy of Chemical Substances" and the book[78] "Valence and the Structure of Atoms and Molecules" both appeared. These two subjects will be given individual sections; the work on heavy hydrogen, that on color and that an acids and bases will also each be given a section. Still another section covers many of the unrelated papers and the book[93] "The Anatomy of Science".

Thermodynamics Lewis' interest in thermodynamics started with his thesis and went on for over twenty years. The theoretical plan of attack is described in the early 1907 paper[17] "Outlines of a new system of thermodynamic chemistry". This plan was followed rather closely in subsequent work. In this paper the ideas of fugacity and activity are introduced to give precision to equations that had been only approximations in earlier work. The later work in this period included consideration of electrolyte solutions, and there were studies on the activity coefficients of solutions of electrolytes. This intense concentration by Lewis and his colleagues at MIT and then at Berkeley culminated in the 1923 book[77] published with Merle Randall "Thermodynamics and the Free Energy of Chemical Substances". When published, it contained not only the up to date theoretical and practical methods of chemical thermodynamics, but also the very precise experimental results of these many years of effort and those of others. The inclusion of the free energy phrase in the title implies the presence of many connected experimental values and results. Not only was the book an immensely useful tabulation, but it was in use as a text in this country and abroad both in English and in translations throughout the world for more than twenty years. This book is one of the illustrations of Lewis's characteristic writing methods; he would discuss the subject for many days with his coworker, in this case Randall, then he would dictate the paper or chapter in virtually finished form. Memories of hearing this dictation from his office are described by others.

When I came to Rice in 1948, Lewis and Randall was used as the text in thermodynamics twenty five years after its publication and stayed in use for many more years. The fact that it was taught at Rice by John Kilpatrick who got his PhD at Berkeley shows one reason for the continued popularity: Berkeley graduates were spread all over the country by that time, but it was also widely adopted by many others. There have been extensions to many more compounds and less common elements in the intervening years, but the tables remain useful with few major corrections seventy years later.

As widely read and as popular this book was, a warning about the explosive hazard of ammonium nitrate has been ignored. Although generally regarded as a rather safe compound (The Chemical Rubber Handbook lists a melting point and even a boiling point without comment), Lewis and Randall calculate even for a dilute water solution very high negative values of both the free energy and enthalpy for the decomposition into water, nitrogen, and oxygen. They point out that a violent explosion in Brest was attributed to this substance. The disastrous explosion in Texas City in 1947 which virtually destroyed the port with great loss of life arose from a fire on a shipload of this substance; it took place well after the warning in the book.

The use of ammonium nitrate as a component of explosives like metal nitrates had been long known. The mixture of ammonium nitrate with Diesel oil has been for long a known mining explosive and became recently notorious with the Oklahoma City explosion. However, the fact that it was by itself explosive was not widely appreciated even after the rough calculation in Lewis and Randall.

A second edition of "Thermodynamics" with extensive revision by K. S. Pitzer and L. Brewer[217] came out in 1961, which included many of the later theoretical developments, especially about ionic solutions and statistical mechanical treatments. The revision is a very valuable contribution to thermodynamic theory and the tables of thermodynamic functions are greatly expanded. Of course these can no longer claim to be a complete listing of known free energies. Perhaps for that reason the new title is simply "Thermodynamics".

Ken Pitzer, a Latimer PhD who also gave great credit to Giauque, was a member of the faculty starting in 1937. He left in 1949 to become director of research of the atomic energy commission and returned in 1951; he stayed for about ten years before accepting the presidency of Rice University, then that of Stanford University and finally resuming his professorship at Berkeley until his death in '97.

Pitzer contributed to the Las Vegas symposium a paper[218] "Gilbert N. Lewis and the Thermodynamics of Strong Electrolytes". In this he describes Lewis' contributions to the properties of solutions of strong electrolytes, not many years after the existence of substances completely dissociated into ions in solution was becoming accepted. Although extremely dilute solutions of these strong electrolytes did behave like the hypothetical ideal solutions of the independent ions, even modestly concentrated solutions gave inconsistencies between conductivity, osmotic pressure, and freezing point depression. The introduction of activities rather than concentrations formally got rid of the discrepancy between freezing point depressions and osmotic pressure but it did not at first give a method of understanding these activity coefficients. The inconsistency in conductivities was not well understood for many years; since it involves an essentially kinetic phenomenon, the failure to correlate with thermodynamics is easily understood. The measurement of substantial number of activity coefficients, mostly by freezing point methods, gave enough data for qualitative and quantitative empirical treatments. The ionic strength as defined and its use was shown to allow a good approximation to the activity coefficients of solutions at somewhat higher concentrations, but still higher concentrations resisted quantitative treatment. Pitzer emphasizes the point that the empirical equations of Lewis anticipated their theoretical justification later by the Debye and Hückel theory.

Pitzer gives us an interesting personal sidelight:[217] "Since Gibbs died in 1903, not long after Lewis's first paper in 1899, it is not obvious whether they became personally acquainted or not, and I am sorry I never asked Lewis about Gibbs. But E. W. Hughes did ask and thoughtfully gave others a report on the reply which I summarize. Hughes said that the question brought a happy smile and that Lewis said he had stopped over at New Haven on one of his many journeys between his home in New York City and Harvard while he was still a graduate student. Although completely unknown to Gibbs, he was warmly welcomed. Gibbs professed to be rather lonely at Yale where there were few, if any others actively interested in his work. Lewis repeatedly suggested that he should not impose further on the time of the great man but Gibbs kept him engaged in conversation all afternoon. Thus it is clear that Lewis did have at least one long and friendly conversation with Gibbs". The only question that I have about this story is that I have no evidence that my father ever had a home in New York, a long and somewhat expensive way from Cambridge for a graduate student or an instructor.

Lewis collaborated with J. E. Mayer in papers in 1928 and 1929[100, 101, 102, 104] on "Thermodynamics Based on Statistics" and two papers without coauthor on "Generalized" and "More Fundamental" thermodynamics appeared in 1931[107,108] ; they marked the end of his work on chemical thermodynamics. The statistical thermodynamics of course did not appear in Lewis and Randall, but is thoroughly treated in Pitzer and Brewer's second edition.

Valence The seminal 1916 paper[55] "The Atom and the Molecule", introduced the concept of the electron pair bond and the rule of eight. Two other papers[56,60] on atomic and molecular structure are also from this period. It was preceded by a 1913 paper[42], "Valence and Tautomerism", which recognized the difference between ionic bonds and those nonpolar or covalent bonds found in organic molecules, and in fact in all recognizable molecules. These bonds he recognized in the 1916 paper consisting of shared of electron pairs. The 1913 paper was in turn preceded by a paper of the same title "Valence and Tautomerism" published by Bray and Branch[219]. It is an interesting comment on the Berkeley environment that this latter paper was written by a Lewis colleague in collaboration with Branch, Lewis' first graduate student, in his second year at Berkeley.

The 1916 paper excited a great deal of attention world-wide. It was the basis of many papers and lectures by Irving Langmuir, which led to it being called by some the Lewis-Langmuir theory, a name Lewis was unable to refute until his war service was over. The book[78] "Valence and the Structure of Atoms and Molecules" appeared in 1923; it has had a lasting influence especially among organic chemists, and is said to have been written for this refutation. The electron pair bond is to this day an important part of the thinking about bonding in spite of the comment in the preface "I take it that a monograph of this sort belongs to the ephemeral literature of science". The persistence of the ideas is shown by the reissue of "Valence and the Structure of Atoms and Molecules" as a Dover book in 1966 without any revision but with a new introduction again by K. S. Pitzer. The electron pair bond has been from its conception to the present day a remarkably useful qualitative description of bonding, especially in organic molecules, and it is certainly one of the pioneering concepts introduced by Lewis. The paired electron bond had an immense influence and enormously helped the influential and ground-breaking study and description of organic mechanisms and structure by Ingold, Hughes and their University College, London, group and later by chemists everywhere. The book also describes the special properties of molecules which violate the rule of eight. Rearrangements of electron deficient molecules and the fascinating properties of free radicals owe much of their present understanding to ideas presented in the book.

The book defined generalized acids, molecules capable of sharing a pair of electrons from a generalized base supplying an unshared pair to create a new bond. These acids and bases (now called Lewis acids and Lewis bases) differed in a major way from the proton and hydroxide ion centered definitions in use at the time. The further development of the ideas came many years later. They are presented in another section.

Although Lewis claimed to have had these ideas much earlier, as shown for example by the reproduction of the pictures of cubic atoms from an old note book in the "Valence" book, nothing appeared in print until the 1913 paper that clarified the distinction between polar and nonpolar molecules. The 1916 paper then almost completed the description of bonds, including double and triple bonds. It was necessary in order to accommodate the triple bond to modify the cube by putting the electrons in pairs on alternate edges of the cube, thus giving it the structure of the regular tetrahedron with an electron pair on each corner, and reconciling the electron pair bond with the organic chemists' evidence from stereochemistry.

There is a considerable discussion of the magnetism of molecules, mostly of diamagnetism which has not since been a very useful tool in molecular structure. However there is the observation that odd molecules must be paramagnetic, a concept much used later in the study of organic free radicals. There is the observation of the paramagnetism of oxygen, and the suggestion (not since accepted) that this is a general property of the double bond. However the concept that the electron magnets are neutralized in the electron pairs, either shared or unshared, is central to the later treatment of bonding.

The publication of "Valence" in the same year as the thermodynamics book is an impressive demonstration of both his writing skill and his ability to think about two unrelated areas at the same time. It has been suggested that this book was published to regain some of the initiative lost to Langmuir during the war. Certainly Lewis first was gratified by Langmuir's acceptance of his ideas but later came to resent the development of the theory under the name Lewis-Langmuir theory or even just Langmuir theory. A statement from the book on Langmuir's contribution is one of the milder things that he had to say on the subject:

"It has been a cause of much satisfaction to me to find that in the course of this series of applications of the new theory, conducted with the greatest acumen, Dr. Langmuir has not been obliged to change the theory which I advanced. Here and there he has been tempted to regard certain rules or tendencies as more universal in their scope than I considered them in my paper, or than I now consider them, but these questions we shall have a later opportunity to discuss. The theory has been designated in some quarters as the Lewis-Langmuir theory, which would imply some sort of collaboration. As a matter of fact, Dr. Langmuir's work has been entirely independent, and such additions as he has made to what was stated or implied in my paper should be credited to him alone."

An article "Abegg, Lewis, Langmuir, and the Octet Rule" by William B. Jensen in the Lewis symposium[220] traces the valence ideas of Abegg to the electron ones of Kossel and of Lewis and the development of these ideas by Langmuir. The term "octet" was a creation of Langmuir, but the number eight as the sum of the maximum and minimum valences was shown to be a much older concept, originating even with Mendeleev. The eight electrons did suggest the cubical atom, which Lewis apparently visualized in 1902, but did not publish until much later. Langmuir failed to account for the triple bond and was led to some outré structures for molecules like N_2. Another useful source for the development of the electron

pair bond is the article by Kohler.[221] Similarly, in the symposium, Stranges[222] also traces the development of the idea of the electron pair bond starting with the early electrostatic theories up to Lewis's complete description in 1916, but does not give as much credit to Thompson and to Parson as Kohler does.

Linus Pauling knew G. N. Lewis since the late 1920s. This was a longer time than anyone else participating in the Lewis symposium with the exception of my brother. Pauling's contribution[223] to the symposium not only is a discussion of the chemical bond in the light of Lewis and later developments, but it also has personal comments related to the long friendship. During most of Lewis's Berkeley career California was remote from the rest of the country, with travel to the East coast requiring several days on several trains. The rest of California was more easily accessible, one day or one night on the train would get one to Cal Tech or back, and Stanford was reached in a few hours by car. Lewis' former leader at MIT, A. A. Noyes, came to Pasadena and was instrumental in establishing a chemistry department at the newly named California Institute of Technology, becoming chairman of the departments of chemistry and chemical engineering in 1921. Pauling had applied to Berkeley for graduate school, but wasn't given a reply fast enough in the face of a Cal Tech offer[201]. There were close relations between the Berkeley and Pasadena departments, but not without some problems. Pauling was awarded a National Research Council fellowship at Berkeley, but according to his symposium paper, he resigned this to take a Guggenheim fellowship in Europe. However, according to Jolly's book[201], Noyes persuaded Pauling to go to Europe rather than Berkeley. It appears that Noyes tried to keep Pauling away from Berkeley until he was well established at Cal Tech and could be kept out of the Lewis clutches.

Pauling did spend time later at Berkeley for 1-2 months each year as a visiting lecturer for five years starting in '29, and got to know Lewis and his family well in this time. I remember Pauling first from this time. Pauling credited Lewis with the electron pair bond and the recognition of partial ionic character in single bonds, but gave more credit to Langmuir than Lewis did for concepts such as "isosterism" in which molecules or ions with the same number of heavy elements and the same number of electrons had the same structure, molecules which now would be called isoelectronic. This idea led to correct structures of CO_2, N_2O, NCO^- and NNN^-, but some other structures were wrong. Lewis did not use resonance, even though he was concerned about the threefold symmetry of the carbonate ion, which had been demonstrated by an early X-ray diffraction. Calvin[224] quotes from the 1916 paper to the effect that Lewis recognized that a structure could be in between two alternative structures, now called contributing structures, but apparently did not, except by implication, appreciate the major stabilization associated with ambiguity, which is now called resonance. Pauling had a very high opinion of Lewis, he said that the 1916 paper revolutionized chemistry. He said that Lewis with

Parson anticipated by 25 years the discovery that the electron has spin and a magnetic moment, although the idea was not exploited. Perhaps the most sincere indication of Pauling's admiration is that his book, "The Nature of the Chemical Bond", was dedicated to Gilbert Newton Lewis.

Heavy water The mass 2 isotope of hydrogen, called deuterium, was discovered by Urey (a Lewis PhD) in 1932. Starting in 1933 there came an extraordinary series of papers[110-135] on the isolation of heavy water and other deuterium compounds and their properties. The first paper on "The Isotope of Hydrogen"[110] was followed by a paper on the concentration of ^2H (deuterium) isotope by water electrolysis with R. T. Macdonald[111], and then by a series of papers on isotopic separations, nuclear properties of deuterium as an ion in the cyclotron beam, the properties of heavy water, the biological properties of heavy water, properties of DCl, of CH_3COOD, of D_2, of DCN, and the properties of D_2O as a solvent. In all there were 26 papers in 1933 and 1934 on these subjects. Nearly all this work was done with very small amounts of heavy water, and special microchemical techniques were developed. The area was abruptly dropped after this initial spurt, except that the related partial separation of the lithium isotopes was published[138] in 1936.

Jacob Bigeleisen was one of Lewis's last students. His work with Lewis did not involve isotopes, but he is now best known for his extensive and definitive work on isotope effects. His symposium paper[225] is entitled "Gilbert N. Lewis and the Beginning of Isotope Chemistry". He describes a chemical method used for separation of lithium isotopes and separation of O^{18} and O^{16} by distillation. The separation of hydrogen and deuterium by the repeated electrolysis of water gave an exceedingly small amount of nearly pure D_2O; later, fractional distillation followed by electrolysis gave somewhat larger amounts, up to about 1g every week. Lewis used it for the study of the physical and chemical properties of heavy water and other compounds containing deuterium, and to supply deuterium to other laboratories throughout the world.

Bigeleisen compares many of the results, especially on vapor pressure to those made more recently, and the agreement is remarkable considering that the amount of material available was minuscule and the isotopic purity of some of the samples was in question because of exchange on glassware. The vapor pressure studies included the comparison of those of H_2 and D_2, both liquid and solid. A search[114] was made for ^3H in concentrated D_2 by spectroscopic methods, but none was found. I remember looking through the spectroscope for the predicted line, but like more experienced spectroscopists I saw nothing. Later, Libby (a Berkeley PhD) found tritium in water newly obtained from the atmosphere at very low concentrations by its feeble beta radiation.[226] Here as in the deuterium case extensive concentration by electrolysis reminiscent of the heavy water isolation was usually used before the sample could be counted. Studies on the dissociation of deuterated weak acids were undertaken with results close to those more recently obtained. Bigeleisen notes that in this work, all carried out on 1 ml or less, the aim was not to get the most accurate result possible, which could be done by others later, but to get preliminary values that could help direct further work. The spin of the deuterium nucleus was found to be 1 from the rotational structure of the molecular spectrum of D_2. There were experiments on animal and vegetable life showing that D_2O was toxic, but these were limited by the amounts available. In collaboration with E. O. Lawrence some nuclear reactions using accelerated deuterium ions were explored using the early cyclotron. This collaboration with E. O. Lawrence to study some of the nuclear reactions of deuterium is an example of Lewis's broad interests as well as his willingness to collaborate with experts in another field.

Everyone noting Lewis's work comments on the complete cessation of deuterium studies after only two years of intense and highly productive work. It has been suggested that this work represented an effort to convince the Nobel prize committee in Stockholm that more than one prize on deuterium could be given. I have no information on whether there is any basis for this idea, and never heard my father talk about the prize.

Bigeleisen also has some comments about working for Lewis. When accepted as a Lewis student, he was asked to give "a commitment to work seven days a week, approximately 14 hours a day!....". How many students would a current professor get with such demands? Bigeleisen's production of eight papers from his PhD work suggests that he must have taken this instruction seriously in his two years at Berkeley. None of this work was on isotopes, which was all finished well before he got to Berkeley, yet his development into now the elder statesman of isotope effects suggests that some of the excitement over isotopes must have lingered in the atmosphere. He does admit to having access to old notebooks and being instructed to destroy them, which he did, but not before reading them.

The number of students, assistants, and faculty coworkers who contributed to

38

the deuterium work was large compared to that of the earlier Lewis work, thus there were 11 different coauthors of 26 papers on deuterium in two years, about 5.5 per year. In other periods there were about 1-3 different coauthors per year, the difference can be attributed in part to the difficult and varied experimental techniques employed in the deuterium work, and in part to the high level of activity leading to many papers in this short time.

Acids and Bases. Lewis presented[143] the Franklin Medal address in 1938. It was an oral presentation, with colorful demonstrations, on "Acids and Bases". It represented a return to a theme touched on more briefly in the "Valence" book. The definition of an acid as a molecule having an insufficiency of electrons that could form a bond with a molecule with an unshared pair of electrons (a base) by sharing that pair contrasted to the water-centered view promoted by Brønsted that an acid was a molecule that could donate a proton to a base. The term Lewis Acid is still in extensive use, although the term Lewis base is less used. The Lewis base, with its unshared electron pair, is by this definition related to the acid definition. However, all Lewis bases are Brønsted bases, and all Brønsted bases are Lewis bases, so generally only the term base is used. Several papers[144, 145 147] with G. T. Seaborg explored other aspects of organic acids and bases. "Primary" acids and bases and "Secondary" ones were distinguished because the secondary ones reacted more slowly and had a measurably large activation energy.

Glenn Seaborg was Lewis's assistant from 1937 to '39, having completed his degree in nuclear chemistry with Gibson. He describes[227] in "The Research Style of Gilbert N. Lewis" their collaboration on acids and bases. An article[228] "Gilbert Newton Lewis - Some Personal Recollections of a Chemical Giant" by Seaborg also contributed to this biography.

Seaborg describes how he came to this position as Lewis's assistant. "I had completed my graduate research [with Gibson] in the spring of 1937, my PhD had been awarded, and it was time for me to go and find a job someplace. Lewis didn't recommend me for a position anywhere, which I could have regarded as a bad sign. Actually, in this case it was a good sign. That meant that I still had a chance to stay at Berkeley in some capacity– which, of course was my objective. One day in July when the next academic year had actually started (so I was technically without any salary), Lewis called me into his office and asked me if I would like to be his research assistant. Lewis was unique in having a personal research assistant, whose salary at that time was $1800 per year. Although I fervently wanted to stay in some capacity, I was flabbergasted to find he thought me qualified for this role, and I expressed my doubts to him. He smiled and indicated that if he didn't think I could do the job he wouldn't have offered it to me. My acceptance of the position he offered was enthusiastic, and thus our two-year intimate association began"

Their research consisted of a study of the reactions of acids with bases in the sense of bond formation, done in solvents not containing ionizable protons. The experiments involved looking at the color changes of a series of indicators in the presence of compounds still almost universally referred to as Lewis acids, such as anhydrous stannic chloride, boron chloride and sulfur dioxide, and the same indicators in the presence of Lewis bases such as triethyl amine. These experiments were essentially done in test tubes without concern for atmospheric and water contamination. They also observed that they could reverse the color change induced by an acid by adding a base. Seaborg illustrates this section with transcripts of his research notebook and with photographs of the notebook pages.

Seaborg noted: "I was immediately struck by the combination of simplicity and power in the Lewis research style, and this impression grew during the entire period of my work with him. He disdained complex apparatus and measurements. He reveled in uncomplicated but highly meaningful experiments. And he had the capability to deduce a maximum of information, including equilibrium and heat of activation data from our elementary experiments. I never ceased to marvel at his reasoning power and ability to plan the next logical step towards our goal. I learned from him habits of thought that were to aid continuously my subsequent scientific career. And, of course working – and apparently holding my own – with him boosted my self-confidence, which was not at a very high level at this stage of my life".

These results were enough to provide lecture demonstrations for Lewis's talk before the Franklin Institute in Philadelphia, and Seaborg tells about trying to pack the chemicals and the equipment needed for these demonstrations for the trip to Philadelphia in the small space left over in two suitcases already nearly filled with the large number of necessary boxes of cigars. After his return with the Franklin Medal the acid-base work continued. There were more careful experiments using very dry solvents, avoidance of protic indicators and vacuum line techniques to avoid contamination by water or other protic acids; the results were the same as in the test tube experiments.

The study continued with some interesting work on slow processes in the reactions of trinitrotriphenylmethane and its anion with acids and bases. These slow processes were identified as those of secondary acids or bases. The activation energy of this slow secondary acid reaction was measured. Further work involved nitrobenzene derivatives as secondary acids.

While this work with Lewis was going on, Seaborg also continued his work in nuclear chemistry, which became his major interest after his time with Lewis. It is not necessary to state that this was a fruitful research, for Seaborg's subsequent career in this field leading to the isolation of plutonium and other transuranic elements and a Nobel prize is well known, as is the still further work on heavier elements and also a ten year term as chairman of the Atomic Energy Commission. The naming of element 106 as "Seaborgium", Sg, was at one time controversial but now the name appears to be settled.

Leo Brewer, who also was concerned with acids and bases, was a graduate student with Olson during Lewis's last years as an administrator and joined the faculty in 1946. He later was coauthor with Pitzer of the second edition of "Thermodynamics" He contributed an article [229] to the Lewis symposium "The Generalized Lewis-Acid-Base Theory: Surprising Recent Developments." In it he notes that although he did both undergraduate and graduate work in aspects of organic chemistry, he got a very broad exposure. This enabled him to get into the wide areas of inorganic and high temperature chemistry that he has since pursued. He joined the faculty just after Lewis' death, but he appreciated the Lewis acid-base theory to an extent that he found that it applied to metallic interactions among the d electrons that closely follow the Lewis acid-base theory developed for what turned out to be called s and p electrons. The energies involved in these interactions are very large; an example quoted is the extremely stable compound of zirconium and platinum.

Color. Color was a subject of interest and fascination to Lewis from the beginning. In a paper[6] from Manila, "Hydration in Solution", the colors of water solutions of copper and cobalt chloride and bromide were used to draw some conclusions about the hydration of these two cations. This was extended in another paper[11]. In the well known 1916 paper[55], the idea of the contribution of electron mobility to color was first introduced, to be elaborated in the "Valence" book[78]. A paper on color and chemical constitution[72] was about the last before his interest in color changed to organic substances, rather than inorganic ones. One can guess that the developing interest in organic materials may have originated from the intensely colored organic indicators that Lewis, Seaborg and Bigeleisen used in their work.

Calvin describes[224] how he collaborated with Lewis on a review[146] on "The Color of Organic Substances". This was apparently a form of examination to see if

Calvin was really worthy of a Berkeley appointment. Apparently he passed this examination, for he was given tenure and continued a distinguished career including an emphasis on photosynthesis, for which he was awarded the Nobel prize in 1961.

The review contained a treatment of essentially linear polyenes as one-dimensional harmonic oscillators, an early quantum mechanical problem. Absorption spectra at first were determined from photographic images of the spectrum, next to an iron spectrum for wave length calibration. The length, that is the number of connected conjugated double bonds, was correlated with the absorption spectrum in fair agreement with the theory. Many dyes are not reasonably considered as linear systems only, several are nearly planar. Light absorption bands attributable to electronic oscillation perpendicular to the long dimension (y bands), or even one further dimension (z bands) in certain dyes which polymerized normal to the molecular plane were identified.

Kasha[230] describes how a series of entirely new near infrared absorption bands were discovered that were finally shown to be an artifact due to a malfunction in the spectrophotometer, a new Beckman DU, giving support to Lewis's distrust of complex equipment.

Later work, much with Bigeleisen, on the absorption spectra of dyes dissolved in glassy solvents at low temperatures showed the light absorption to be much sharper and frequently accompanied by fluorescence and sometimes phosphorescence. The preparation of these glasses was a special trick, especially with the room temperature boric acid glasses. Lewis made these himself, not trusting anyone else to do it properly. It was originally thought that the phosphorescence was due to the rigid environment, but this turned out not to be necessary. Culminating this work was the identification of the phosphorescent state with the lowest triplet state[162] with his last student, Michael Kasha. The final paper[165], with Calvin on "Paramagnetism of the Phosphorescent State" confirmed the identification of this state as a triplet by showing that it was paramagnetic. Some initial experimental problems arose from the presence of paramagnetic oxygen in the magnetic field. This anomaly was resolved by a corridor conversation[231] with professor Giauque; such conversations were facilitated by the structure of Gilman Hall and they helped solve many problems. This study was based on the earlier conclusion by Lewis that molecules with unpaired electrons should be paramagnetic. This paper was of great impact on the photochemical community and is still regarded as a classic. This was the last experimental paper that Lewis wrote, although his name appears on a paper, with Calvin and Kasha[168] written after his death, on a refinement of this study of the paramagnetism of the triplet state. In his symposium talk, Kasha[230] describes the difficulty of getting general acceptance of the idea of a triplet state which was the phosphorescent state. After the magnetic work, Kasha[232] spent years accumulating further evidence.

Michael Kasha contributed the last paper[230] of the symposium, "The Triplet State: An Example of G. N. Lewis' Research Style." Kasha was Lewis's last graduate student; he worked on the fluorescence and phosphorescence problem. In the paper he traces the development of the idea of triplet states and the unallowed transitions between states of different multiplicity. The identification of the triplet state as the phosphorescent one was a consequence of this development, an identification confirmed by the above observation of the paramagnetism of the phosphorescent state. Kasha continued this study and obtained quantitative results on the magnetic moment of this state in a paper with Calvin published after Lewis's death[168]. He was also able to observe absorption spectra leading to the triplet state directly, and also observe further excitation of the lowest triplet state. Kasha describes how the idea of the triplet phosphorescent state was poorly received and was ignored for years. It took a great deal of further work from his own lab. at Tallahassee[232] and from others to be unequivocally convincing and to lead to the ultimate acceptance of this view. It is now hard to understand the reluctance of reputable chemists to accept this concept. This identification of the phosphorescent state with the triplet state is surely another of the pioneering advances made by Lewis.

Kasha also noted a trend in Lewis's research: he would write a review of a field before his research started. Several examples are to be found. The long series of papers on thermodynamics were preceded by the important paper "Outlines of a New System of Thermodynamic Chemistry," published in 1907. The atomic and electronic structures appear, according to Kasha, to have originated in his 1898 Master's thesis "The Electron and the Molecule" which seems to have completely disappeared, and the confirmation even of the title of this thesis is lacking. As mentioned above, the failure to refer to this[55] in "The Atom and the Molecule", which does have a reference to pictures of the cubical atoms taken from a 1902 notebook sketch, suggests that a better reference does not exist. The subject of the MA thesis remains a unknown. The 1916 paper also rearranges the electrons at the corners of the cube to a tetrahedral arrangement of electron pairs on the edges of the cube, which not only allowed the visualization of triple bonds, but also reconciledthe electron pair structures to the tetrahedral symmetry required by optical activity and the stereochemical studies of van't Hoff and Lebel. This paper and the book are necessary precursors to the later work on acids and bases, but the field was introduced by a paper[143] "Acids and Bases" in 1938. All the work on color was introduced by a review[146] with Calvin "The Color of Organic Substances". The heavy water work was not preceded by such a review, since heavy water was not available before his own work in this area.

Kasha comments on Lewis's style of research in which the late morning was devoted to making experimental plans for the afternoon, with enough to do to keep his assistant or graduate student occupied for many hours, sometimes days. Both Kasha and Seaborg have commented on this timetable, and it was apparently much more general than that. He would come in afternoons to work in the lab, having no further administrative duties by the time Kasha came.

In the afternoon of the 23d of March in 1946 Kasha was working in another room, and came into Lewis' lab to find him on the floor surrounded by a potent smell of hydrogen cyanide, and a broken ampule of liquid hydrogen cyanide was near him where he was lying. Kasha quickly opened the window to dispel the fumes, but it was too late. Lewis was dead on arrival at the hospital, later determined to have had a heart attack, and confirmed by an autopsy. The cyanide was apparently dropped after the almost instantaneous death.

Jolly[201] suggested his death was suicide, and some older faculty members also had this idea earlier that death was a result of self-administered cyanide poisoning. The basis of this suggestion was a perception of melancholy following the end of the war and a deterioration of health. I did not detect melancholy two months earlier, but of course I did not see him after that. Deterioration of health is consistent with a natural death. The presence of the vial of hydrogen cyanide was not remarkable, since Lewis had very recently expressed an interest in this as a solvent of quite high dielectric constant. The evidence for cyanide poisoning would surely have been found in the autopsy, performed because he had had no regular doctor for a long time. Furthermore, suicide was to me and many others totally out of character; I did not hear this proposed until reading Jolly's book and was shocked and incredulous. My mother never told me about this suggestion, and may never even have heard about it.

Thus ended suddenly an amazingly productive and varied career as a chemist, scientist, and a leader and stimulator of his numerous highly distinguished colleagues, assistants, and graduate students.

Of all Lewis's later students and assistants, Kasha was the one most directly influenced in his subsequent work, and he published papers supporting the triplet phosphorescent state for several years before it was finally widely accepted.

In another paper[232] Kasha says "He confessed to me that organic molecules had been his special joy in his later years, and how because he had failed a course in organic chemistry at Harvard as a student he had developed a life-time dislike of organic molecules - much to his later regret and chagrin". This statement did not come as a surprise to me for he told me (it must have been about the same time) that he was very excited about the work he was doing on these fluorescent and phosphorescent substances and looking back he did not understand why he had spent so much time working on an area "as dull as thermodynamics!"

The Anatomy of Science and other areas. Three years after the two books above [77,78] a third book [93] "The Anatomy of Science" was published. This was based on the Silliman lectures given at Yale, a rather rare example of a major oral presentation. It is a very difficult book to discuss here, partly because it is written in a more philosophical tone than the others, partly because it covers a vast range of subjects, and partly because I have had difficulty finding any evidence that it had a major influence on science. The lectures were given before a lay audience, so perhaps one should not expect any major consequences. It presents science of that day with some amusing examples. It included a plausible if improbable development of counting. It develops the idea of non-Euclidean geometry by telling about mythical South Sea islanders who found that to get to a distant island due east it was shorter to go by way of a more southerly island than going straight east. The shortest path they found was to us the great circle route, but since they did not know that they were living on a spherical surface, they just modified the geometry.

Newtonian mechanics was shown to be supplanted by special relativity but only when very high speeds were involved and once again the geometry had to change. The problem of gravitation and its effect to distort the geometry was recognized, but the quantitative treatment was not attacked. The lectures included recognition of the quantum nature of light and other optics; probability and entropy were discussed, including the relation between the reversibility of time which appears in all the equations of physics of few particles but contravenes the second law of thermodynamics which is related to very large numbers of particles.

A next to the last chapter is on the nonmathematical sciences. Lewis had recognized but did not subscribe to the existence of a caste system among those who hold that there is a hierarchy of sciences with mathematics at the top and most respectable, then physics, then chemistry, with biology near the bottom, which at the time of writing was almost wholly nonmathematical and therefore hardly respectable from this point of view. Organic chemistry is therefore an inferior part of chemistry, yet a section on optical activity pointing out the absence of this activity in ordinary synthetically produced organic molecules and its near universal presence in natural products does show a problem not covered by the simple application of mathematics or even physical chemistry. At the bottom of this hierarchy, almost an untouchable caste, are the purely observational sciences. However, Lewis includes a discussion of animal (including insects) behavior contrasted with that of man. He recognized the problem of distinguishing between the adaptation of animals to changes in environment and those related to a real inheritable change leading to a permanent new characteristic.

The tone of the work becomes increasingly philosophical as it advances. The last chapter, "Life; Body and Mind", takes Lewis far from his background of rigorous thermodynamics and the mathematics of relativity and of quantum mechanics. It is hard to look at this over seventy years later without putting in ideas which were not then developed. He considers that the intellectual feats of man may be a consequence of his ability to store knowledge, not in his brain, but in books and art. The concept of inheritance of acquired characteristics is one, now forbidden, that he is attracted to, but eventually does reject. He ends up finding himself forced to accept free will, even though there is still opposition to it.

Reading of this book is still a challenging experience; I do not know if my own reaction is colored by my inferior knowledge of philosophy or by the changes in scientific ideas over the intervening years.

G. N. Lewis was far from a specialist. Although his work in each of the areas covered in the earlier sections of this chapter would have sufficed to gain him wide renown, even the sum of all these does not describe his breadth of interest. He published papers in many areas not closely related to the main themes of his life work. Some of these are scientifically important, some are creative ideas which were not followed up, and some represented imaginative ideas which have not stood the test of time. I mention these because they show his wide ranging and sometimes fanciful mind with the comment that the best of creative ideas are often preceded by those which may be wildly far-flung and not always sound.

His appreciation of relativity started early, well before there was acceptance in the scientific community, shown in papers up to 1912[20,24,25,38, and 50].

Lewis' paper on four-dimensional vector analysis[29] was not followed up, yet it showed that he was comfortable with this level of mathematics. Two papers on quantum theory [43,50] shows him getting his feet wet in this subject. His idea of "ultimate rational units" [43,76] and [86] which appears first here, has been found wanting. A paper on the chemistry of the stars and the origin of elements [75] is quite early in the thinking of such ideas. He left chemistry and physics in two papers [83,85] on monetary policy; it is not clear whether these papers were read at all by economists.

A series of papers on light faced the problem of the wave or corpuscular nature of light included an attack [88] on the Planck radiation law which was roundly criticized in a letter from Einstein. This forced Lewis to abandon some, but not all of his ideas on the conservation of photons [94], which was based on the idea that emission of radiation could only occur if an absorber was also present. Some of this work attracted much attention in the popular press. Thus he is reported [204] to have said that Julius Caesar's decision to cross the Rubicon depended on our present actions, a result of the idea that the emission of a light quantum did not occur until it could be absorbed elsewhere. This was quoted more than once, but I have not found the original. The equations of physics are symmetrical with respect to time; it can go either forward or backward, yet we have an instinct of a one-way passage of time. The second law of thermodynamics, the law which states that the entropy of the universe is constantly increasing, offers a way out of this dilemma. The problem is discussed in "The Anatomy of Science".

A paper [99] looks at the possibility of attributing all the mutations leading to the variation of species to natural radioactivity. Although some mutations definitely arise from radiation, it did not survive later scrutiny. A series of papers [139, 140, 141] on the refraction of neutrons was shown to be experimentally flawed. In fact the flaw was pointed out by Seaborg, [227] who suggested that his comments supported by a simple demonstration helped convince Lewis that he ought to abandon neutron diffraction and to take Seaborg on as a private assistant.

It will be seen that many of the above papers came in a hiatus after a major push in one of the more recognized areas of study and research. Another such a hiatus occurred in the forties. The major work [148-165] on spectra and photochemistry was over by the early summer of 1945. It should not be concluded that the quality of work declined in his later years. The work with Kasha on fluorescence and phosphorescence[162,164, 165, 168] culminated in the identification of the phosphorescent state as the triplet state. The confirmation of this by the demonstration that the phosphorescent state was paramagnetic in the paper with Calvin [165,168] was quite as important as any of his other work.

He did suffer from a diminution of interactions with his colleagues, nearly all of whom were heavily involved with Second World War work, an area in which Lewis did not participate significantly. The publication of all chemical papers was much smaller in 1944 and 1945, an indication of the paucity of unclassified chemistry going on. It is not surprising that a man with an active mind without the opportunity to carry on much chemical research would turn to problems in apparently neglected other fields. I do not know when he started thinking about glaciation and about American anthropology, but he talked to me about these, especially the anthropology, while I was in electronics school for many months and again near Christmas of '45, just before I left the Berkeley area for the last time before his death. I learned much more than I now remember about the origins of American vegetables in this period. However, the varied native languages remained a mystery. He did a great deal of reading on both glaciation and anthropology for months before this time; his bedroom at home was a mass of assorted journals and books. I presume that his office was likewise cluttered with literature on these two subjects.

The last two papers that he wrote were published posthumously. They show how his mind was active to the end and still not averse to attacking conventional wisdom with thoughtful and irreverent suggestions. The first[166] is "The Thermodynamics of an Ice Age: The Cause and Sequence of Glaciation". In this paper processes related to the low albido of ice and snow are postulated which can lead to an accelerated growth of glaciers with a corresponding cooling and drying of the atmosphere, eventually reaching a maximum of glaciation which then spontaneously recedes. The trigger for this process is still obscure. In contrast to some earlier theories, this one is compatible with thermodynamics, in that it does not require the earth to have a memory of the distant past; weather is determined only by the current state.

The second[167] is "The Beginning of Civilization in America". In this latter article, evidence is marshalled to show that the various neolithic arts, such as agriculture, pottery, early metallurgy, arithmetic and astronomy were only invented once, and that these inventions originated in America. The antiquity of the civilization is supported by the great variety of native American languages, an argument which has been brought up again, and the great variety of cultivated crops not found in the wild state. While this thesis has not been widely accepted, the arguments showing ever earlier dates of American civilization are becoming more acceptable as archeological research continues. The paradigm of American anthropology has been that the Clovis men of about ten t o eleven thousand years ago was the first American culture with neolithic skills; men with these then spread rapidly to Central and South America. Recently, since Lewis's paper, there has been evidence of other independent civilizations. An example is the discovery[233] of early man in Brazilian caves in the rain forest, which according to varied dating methods are of about the same age, ten to eleven thousand years ago, as the earliest Clovis sites, but appear to differ greatly in the style of the stone tools and of living. The sites may be even older than Clovis, but that conclusion is not certain. A more recent report of a pre-Clovis site in Monte Verde, Chile, has also been published.[234] This Brazilian discovery has generated considerable controversy, some is summarized in a recent Science magazine,[234] as has the longer known Monte Verde site.

In "Kon-Tiki" Thor Heyerdahl[235] showed that it was possible to cross the Pacific to Polynesia in a balsa raft, such as were used by the Chilean and Peruvian Indians. He considered this strong support for the population of Polynesia and possibly much more of Asia from America. While this thesis is not widely supported, it suggests at least that Lewis's paper was read, and confirmed that transpacific contact was possible.

Lewis did not have any war work contracts, nor did he participate in the work of others. However, it should not be concluded that he was totally out of touch with what was going on. In the spring of 1940 I applied to Harvard for graduate school with the intent of studying organic chemistry. He told me that if I was interested I could probably stay at Berkeley for there was some important inorganic chemistry going on there, and I was probably qualified since I had taken Bray's famous Chem. 120. I had heard about nuclear fission because it was mentioned in a nuclear physics course taught by professor Alvarez, who was very excited about it and the enormous amount of energy released in fission. The subject was almost immediately classified after few lectures and nothing further was said about it in the open. My father was aware of both uranium fission and preliminary plutonium work and couldn't tell me more, beyond the suggestion that there was a promising area of inorganic research being carried out at Berkeley. I think it was good for me to get away and so do not regret ignoring this possibility, although being in at the earliest stages on fission, nuclear energy, and the bombs might have been very exciting. I have never regretted doing physical organic chemistry, indeed, I believe Lewis might have been as fascinated with the subject as I was and still am.

Chapter VII Lewis as Administrator.

From 1912 until 1941 Lewis was Chairman of the Department of Chemistry as well as Dean of the College of Chemistry (an administrative arrangement existing hardly anywhere else but not created by Lewis; it was already in place when he came to California) The evidence of the efficacy of his administration is not seen in vast paper records or in large numbers of assistants. Seaborg writes in his symposium article:[227] "[His] positions would ordinarily entail heavy administrative duties, but he did not allow himself to be burdened by them. Nevertheless, I believe, that he discharged his responsibilities very well. He was efficient and decisive, highly respected by the faculty members in the College, and eminently fair in his dealings them. To a large extent he ran the College from his laboratory. I recall that his efficient secretary, Mabel Kittredge, would come into our laboratory, stand poised with her notebook until she commanded his attention, describe clearly and briefly the matter that required his attention or decision. Lewis would either give his answer immediately or ask her to come back in a little while, after he had given the matter some more thought. This system worked very well in those days [late 1930s]...." A comment on the way people view things is that this same quotation was used by Jolly[201] to bolster the argument that Lewis was an ineffective administrator. It is certainly true that Lewis did not over administer the College or Department, but one must judge the methods by their results.

The level of organization and administrative effectiveness must have been more than adequate as seen in retrospect. The College of Chemistry was virtually unknown outside of California when Lewis arrived, yet within a year graduate students were coming from from distant parts as well as some with Berkeley bachelors degrees. These included several of those who later joined the faculty, such as G. E. K. Branch (from the West Indies, via Edinburgh and Liverpool), C. W. Porter, T. D. Stewart, E. D. Eastman, A. R. Olson, and W. M. Latimer (from University of Kansas), all before 1920. Others of note who were awarded the PhD before 1930 included F. R. v. Bichowsky, W. H. Rodebush, H. E. Bent, T. R Hogness, W. F. Giauque, M. L. Huggins, G. Glockler, G. K. Rollefson, H. C. Urey, O. K. Rice, J. O. Halford, H. Eyring, J. E. Mayer, F. D. Rossini, F. H. Spedding, as well as others whose names I did not immediately recognize. These names are derived from a tribute to Gilbert Newton Lewis[202] published by the

University of California in honor of his seventieth birthday, which lists all his publications to that date, and all the PhDs given by the department between 1914 and 1945. It is clear that the department was attracting graduate students of a high caliber who contributed to faculties at other universities as well as Berkeley in far less than twenty years after Lewis arrived. In the earlier more than thirty years of the department there had been little distinction, but distinction came rapidly and has not slowed since. Many of the new faculty were selected for the National Academy of Sciences (including Lewis, more on this elsewhere). Several of the Berkeley products were awarded the Nobel Prize, namely W. F. Giaque, H. C. Urey, W. F. Libby, G. T. Seaborg, and H. Taube. A rigorous selection of graduate students was of course helped by the magic of California, which at that time was a much more powerful magnet for those with an adventurous spirit than it is now.

The presence of a distinguished department of chemistry was one of the earliest contributors to the reputation of the entire University of California, and Lewis was also a significant factor in the establishment of the academic senate, a powerful elected faculty group. In the academic senate he had a reputation as an opponent not to be taken lightly, and was at the center of controversy often. In sum, while Lewis' administrative style may have been unconventional, one can not argue with success. He was rather autocratic, and in Jolly's words,[201] "he could occasionally show characteristics of arrogance, pomposity and pique." Jolly never met Lewis, but there is some basis from other sources that this statement may be true. As an absolute leader he did delegate some powers to others, thus he put Latimer in charge of student recruiting after several years, and did follow Hildebrand's recommendation on the Calvin appointment.

The university was a catalyst for other universities in the rest of the west coast. Notable among these was Cal Tech; the science departments there were virtually founded by A. A. Noyes. It seems reasonable to conclude that Lewis' success must have helped to influence Noyes to leave his strong position at MIT, where he had appointed Lewis nearly twenty years earlier, and follow him to the wild west. Noyes established a distinguished science group in Pasadena, including a number of years later Linus Pauling. In his book Jolly describes the machinations of Noyes to delay the contact of Pauling with Lewis until he was firmly entrenched at Cal Tech. UCLA became a factor in California science in the thirties, and Stanford was small but had some good people. California, once the frontier, became one of the places to do chemistry. In Lewis' lifetime the center of chemistry moved from Germany to the east coast and then farther west as the California and Midwest impact became felt. It can hardly be claimed that Lewis alone produced this shift, but it cannot be denied that his role was significant.

Lachman[204] believed that the "laissez faire" style of Lewis' administration was far superior to that at several other universities that Lachman visited, and that the open stockroom and availability of keys for all actually was cheaper than the other highly organized systems with formal rules for access and purchasing, administrated by many officers. As an organic chemist, he was impressed by the claim at that time that the stockroom held every organic chemical in the Eastman catalog, each available without charge to any department member, faculty or student. In the more recent times of illicit drug synthesis in private laboratories this would have been harder to justify, but the freedom to use all available sources for research was certainly stimulating.

The success of the Lewis administration rests to a large extent on the standing of the department and the continuing advancement of this standing up to the present time; now it is among the best departments in the world. The spirit started by Lewis has endured among a long series of administrators, including after his death a sequence of faculty that he hired.

GNL's father Frank Lewis is shown here as one of the five Lewis brothers, sons of George Gilbert and Adeline Lewis. It is dated 1867, at which date Frank was already the father of aunt Polly. Frank is therefore at the lower left.

GNL's maternal grandfather, Newton White. It is labelled on the original as "A
very much loved person."

GNL at age three. This is from a Daguerrotype, when this form of photography was disappearing.

GNL's parents and sister, Frank Lewis, Mary Burr White Lewis, and Mary Hannibal Lewis, (Aunt Polly). Since aunt Polly was only nine years older than her brother and she appears to be grown, GNL must have been at least six then.

Gilbert N. Lewis in Lincoln, Nebraska. It was taken in a professional studio and appears to be about the time he was in the University of Nebraska School.

Pach Bros.

935 B'WAY., N.Y.

An authentic picture of G. N. Lewis as Harvard undergraduate.

Above: GNL at Harvard as undergraduate. The identification is uncertain for obvious reasons; it is based on the association with other more certain pictures. Below: Mary Sheldon, shortly before her marriage in 1912.

GNL at sea, probably during his honeymoon in 1912.

Lewis in military uniform, 1918-1919. It is difficult to date this more accurately because his rank is obscured in a black and white photograph since the shoulder insignia for major and lieutenent colonel differ only in the type of metal.

Lewis in military uniform, the chevron on the sleeve suggests that this is a later
picture than the other. Again the rank is unclear. However, here the beard is gone.
There is a beard in the early pictures from Berkeley, sometime after his return from
the army the beard is gone.

Top: The whole Lewis family in Inverness. The children are left to right Ted, Margery and Dick. The early 1920s. Bottom: The Lewis family in the early 1940s on an unremembered festive occasion. Left to right: Ted, Dick, Dick's wife Helen, Mary, Gilbert and Margery. Probably in Berkeley.

ZIONIST ORGANIZATION OF AMERICA

Professor Gilbert Lewis
University of California
Department of Chemistry
Berkeley, California

My dear Professor Lewis:

Please accept my sincere thanks for
your kind letter. It would be a great pleasure for me to
meet you again and also to see your very interesting country.
I am, afraid, however, that it will be impossible for me to
find the necessary time for the very long journey that it would
involve.

As you may be aware I have come to the
United States on a special mission to promote the cause of the
proposed University of Jerusalem and the work in that connection
takes up most of my time, during my stay here which is limited.
Should it happen that somehow a trip to California becomes
possible, I will be very glad indeed to communicate with you
again.

With best regards, I am

Very truly yours,

A. Einstein.

Letter to Lewis from Albert Einstein declining an invitation to visit California.

Top: Meeting in Spain about 1930 at which Lewis was awarded an honorary degree. Talk given by GNL. Below: Formal part of degree ceremony in Madrid. Lewis is the farthest of those in the front row at the left.

Top: GNL at Tomales bay beach with wife Mary and daughter Margery; 1935±2 years. Below: Same at ocean beach with Margery's dog Roguie.

The best known Hagemeyer portrait of Gilbert N. Lewis. It comes from the late 1930s.

A less familiar Hagemeyer portrait of Gilbert N. Lewis contemporaneous with the other familiar one, i.e. late 1930s. Both show the cigar conspicuously.

Mary Lewis, a formal studio portrait by J. Hagemeyer, *ca.* 1940.

Chapter VIII The Research Conference and Lewis as Teacher

Everyone writing on Lewis mentions the weekly research conference. This extraordinary seminar, covering all of chemistry rather than just a small area, does not seem to have an equal in American chemistry then or since. The format does not seem unusual: first a prepared talk from the current literature, presented by a graduate student, then a talk by a graduate student or faculty member on current research within the department. The environment was a little unusual especially by modern standards, it was in a modest sized room with a central table around which the faculty sat surrounded by several rows of chairs for graduate students and other non faculty department members. The room is described as being totally filled with smoke, the largest contributor was Lewis with his chain smoked Phillipine cigars, but there were many others contributing. When someone suggest opening a window, Lewis is quoted[204] as saying "What, and let all this good smoke out?"

An oft quoted story connected with his incessant smoking relates to his use of a lab. with access only through another lab. through which he walked several times a day, carrying the usual lighted cigar. The first lab occupants were working with large amounts of ether and were so terrified about the potential fire that they actually worked up the courage to ask Lewis to stop this hazardous practice. He apologized and thereafter when walking through that lab he held the cigar out of sight behind him. He later demonstrated to me that the hazard was minor (in his opinion) by dropping the ash from his lighted cigar into an open beaker of ether which in several tries never ignited.

Lewis sat in a chair at the end of the table (always the same chair) at the research conference and he and the other faculty would contribute questions to the speaker, whether graduate student or faculty member. Many commented that Lewis could pose hard and relevant questions no matter what the subject of the seminar. Lewis ran this conference in a quite autocratic manner, and some said it was pompous. It was anyway a resounding success. Although I gather that graduate students did not look forward to being so grilled, the ideas presented got a complete going over and many papers were greatly improved by this scrutiny which in other places would have been sent to referees in less polished form. An oft repeated story from Hildebrand is that junior graduate student interrupted with a comment, and Lewis is said to have commented[201] "That is an impertinent comment, but it is also very pertinent." As far as I can tell, this conference declined after Lewis retired, and nothing quite like it has been seen since there or elsewhere in spite of many efforts.

The research conference was a significant teaching device. The description of Lewis as a teacher may at first be hard to understand, for he never met a class at Berkeley, he had a modest number of graduate students, he did not even participate in the freshman lab teaching undertaken by all the rest of the faculty, yet he was recognized as a great teacher by the majority of those in the graduate school.

Gerald Branch wrote an article, included as an appendix by Calvin[219], entitled "Gilbert Newton Lewis, 1875-1946." Branch was the first of Lewis's graduate students. Branch emphasized Lewis as a teacher in spite of his absence from any formal teaching duty. Branch said that Lewis was the creator of text problems for the students, and that this idea caused problem sets to be included in nearly every textbook from the department, with the exception of Branch and Calvin. He attributes the extraordinary success of the PhD graduate to a number of different factors. First was the selection of the students. At the Berkeley department selection was practiced from the Freshman year through the advanced courses which had honors sections. "Natural gifts were considered more important than knowledge of chemistry..... Having chosen a candidate, [Lewis] next made sure that the choice was a happy one, using frequent oral examinations". By assessing the students early the faculty was able to get rid of the final examination for the PhD.

The research conference was an essential part of the teaching of graduate students, and there was much discussion of each talk. Again from Branch: "In these discussions Lewis displayed a depth of insight and brilliance of thought that were an education to all who heard him. He accepted with good grace the harsh criticisms that were characteristic of the conferences. Needless to say his remarks were enlivened by his wit. This wit often pierced to the heart of a problem".

The success of the education was measured by Branch by the great success of the PhDs produced. Many important academic and government positions have been taken by these men and women (The inclusion of women is now politically correct, actually there were only four through 1945). In commenting on the successes, Branch betrays a prejudice which he shared with Lewis: "Strange to say, many have achieved outstanding success in industrial chemistry". In fact, the neglect of applied chemistry, technology and the like was a deliberate policy. Lewis did not approve of industrial consulting and did not permit it to his faculty, he did not have an undergraduate program that put more than minimal emphasis on industrial chemistry, and the department of chemical engineering in the college did not start in earnest until well after he left administrative duties.

The success of Berkeley chemists in the Nobel prize competition has often been noted, and each year the number of lesser prizes awarded to Berkeley chemists continues to rise.

Branch's comments add little new to the life of G. N. Lewis, but I include them for two reasons. My father had respect for each one of his colleagues, but Gerald Branch occupied a unique position at the top of this list, not only for his intellect and chemical prowess but also his extraordinary skill in cards and in chess, at which he was a champion. The comments above show that the esteem was mutual. My reaction to Branch's advanced organic course was extremely favorable, but among the other undergraduates he had a reputation as by far the worst teacher in the department. Of all the faculty that I took courses from, the material of his course stayed with me the longest. When I went to graduate school at Harvard I think I had a better understanding of resonance than any of the other students and my choice of physical-organic chemistry can be traced in part to his influence, even if I was unaware of it at the time. His major interest in structural effects and substituent effects on acid strengths anticipated the Hammett equation by several years.

Branch was not alone in paying tribute to Lewis as a teacher. Here is a paragraph from Harold Urey (Nobel Prize, '34), who left Berkeley immediately after his PhD in 1923. He writes, as quoted by Lachman[204]: "It seems to me that I and many other men owe more of our professional success to Gilbert Lewis than to any other man.... He knew no boundaries of any kind to science.... He was an original thinker and a very vigorous one. But his most important contribution was as a teacher on the highest level."

Willard Libby (again quoted by Lachman) said that Lewis was the finest teacher he had ever known.

A different kind of story about Lewis as a teacher was told me by him, it must date from the time he was an instructor at Harvard. A student came to complain about grading, saying that he knew he had not done well, but how could he get a negative grade? Lewis told him it was because he had made an unnecessary display of ignorance! (This story is also told by Lachman with respect to a Berkeley freshman, an unlikely locale since Lewis never taught freshmen at Berkeley) His later avoidance of classroom teaching becomes more understandable and may show that he knew how he would be received by the undergraduates.

Branch was the among first graduate students to take the PhD with Lewis at Berkeley; there were not a large number who did this and I do not have a complete list. Merle Randall got his PhD with Lewis at MIT. Some other Lewis PhDs were William Argo, Jacob Bigeleisen, T. B. Brighton, Ermon Eastman, Michael Kasha,

W. N. Lacey, Theodore Magel, Joseph Mayer, R. T. Macdonald, Axel Olson and Gerhard Rollefson. Calvin and Seaborg[215] also list several other names as Lewis graduate students: P. Borgstrom, A. L. Caulkins, O. E. Cushman, G. W. Clark, and G. S. Parks. Of these, only Borgstrom and Parks were awarded the PhD, and none appears as a coauthor of a Lewis paper. Some others who published with Lewis, but may not have been his students are Adams and Bichowsky. The exact assignment of research directors is now uncertain, and some sources unreasonably credit Lewis with all the Berkeley PhDs in his period.

The undergraduate education was very carefully planned from the beginning of the freshman year. Lectures were in two sections (of more than 500 each in my time) given with great flair by Hildebrand, and in earlier times by Latimer. The students were placed according to their expected ability in small laboratory sections which met once a week in the Freshman laboratory building, which had many rooms, each for about 25 students. These were, I think unofficially, designated A sections through D sections and the A sections got the best teaching assistants as well as senior faculty for teaching. However, all sections had a member of the faculty who stayed for at least an hour as well as a graduate teaching assistant. Being assigned to one of the lower sections was not necessarily perpetual doom; sections were reassigned for the second semester. This elitist start was very effective, even if it would now be considered politically reprehensible. It was continued into the later years with the establishment of honors courses, allowing the intense exposure to be continued for the best students throughout the undergraduate years. Large numbers of students were always a problem. Even when I was a freshman, the first course had about 1200 students which was almost 10% of the total university undergraduate population, and junior courses had a major influx of junior college transfers, whose prospects were not generally believed to be very good.

I do not know how much of this overall plan is attributable to Lewis, but he organized and controlled the freshman course from his first year in Berkeley. In this connection Lewis denied control of the Freshman course to Professor Morgan, who instantly resigned and went through several appointments before ending up at UCLA, where he did run the Freshman course.[201] Except for being the major influence on the undergraduate curriculum, Lewis had no contact with that program, and when I was there, at least, undergraduates were rather terrified of him. He was protected in his office by Miss Kittredge, herself feared by many undergraduates. I had an exceptional position in that I was not cowed by either of them.

Some aspects of Lewis' research style may be considered part of the education of coworkers. One is his time table, the complete opposite of what he expected of graduate students, although the total time spent was a good example. He would come in to the laboratory quite late, perhaps at ten in the morning, to work in the lab (after his retirement from administration) until about noon, by that time having given his assistant instructions to prepare for the afternoon work. He would then leave for the faculty club, either to eat lunch or just for the society of his friends and the card games, and return to the building at two or three and do the experiments prepared by his assistant (by assistant I mean a colleague, his private assistant or a graduate student). Then, if the family was in Inverness, he might work until late at night. When the experiments had been completed, he would write papers in an individualistic way, he would dictate them in finished form to his assistant. Calvin comments[224] that on one occasion Lewis observed that Calvin didn't write after a sentence was dictated, because he had already written it. This shows that he assembled thoughts from previous discussions using the same words he had spoken before. It also illustrates a point that I had not noticed before: he normally spoke in complete and polished sentences, unlike most of us. This mode of writing is specifically mentioned by Calvin, but it was also used with Randall in writing "Thermodynamics" and there are other mentions of this style.

Chapter IX. The Nobel Prize?

A universal question has been: if Lewis was as distinguished and capable a chemist as everyone says, why did he not win the Nobel prize? There have been many proposed answers to this question. I divide the work many deem worthy of the prize into three areas. First is the work on thermodynamics. Various answers to this question have been proposed.

At the time of greatest thermodynamic output, the appreciation of what Lewis accomplished was very great indeed. Nowadays, everyone takes thermodynamics more or less for granted and the magnitude and relevance of Lewis' accomplishments do not stand out as they did then. Perhaps his contribution was neglected because (at least in some eyes) he seemed to have been so successful in the development of the subject that, in the eyes of some, little new has been done since. This mistaken view has led to its being regarded as a dead field, and therefore not of great worth.

Jolly[201] in his book suggested that to receive the prize for thermodynamics it would have been necessary to have the support of and nomination by Nernst which apparently never came. Nernst himself won the Nobel prize for thermodynamics in 1921. I got the strong impression that my father did not have cordial relations with Nernst although I do not remember the source of this impression. It is possible that my recollection goes only to the time when it was already late for a prize on this subject, perhaps my father felt that Nernst's opposition represented prejudice against him personally and American science in general and responded to this by personal antipathy. In the 1907 paper[17] "Outlines of a New System of Chemical Thermodynamics" there are a few references to Nernst but none that might have been offensive. In the 1913 paper[40] "The Free Energy of Chemical Substances" there is a discussion of the frequent confusion of two terms both called Free Energy (then called A and F) and an example is given of the Nernst book in which on the same page two equations are written which are both wrong because A was used instead of F. I do not know the extent to which this might have contributed to a possible antagonism, but it certainly was not the way to encourage support, a consideration my father would have scorned anyway. Lewis is also said to have spent some of his time in the Phillipines reading and correcting Nernst's text.

With respect to Nernst and the Nobel prize, an advertisement[236] for a forthcoming book on Arrhenius by Elizabeth Crawford, has the following sentences: "Despite a controversialist temperament, friends dominated Arrhenius's life and science. The only exception was the case of Walther Nernst where a close friendship turned to enmity, which led Arrhenius to block Nernst's Nobel prize for some fifteen years." It is therefore not surprising that Nernst would regard Lewis, an iconoclast himself even at that time, as undeserving of the prize in thermodynamics, at least for many years.

In this connection McBryde[237] has written a brief biography "Walther Hermann Nernst" including a summary of Nernst's work. In a concluding section he describes Nernst as "an ingenious, creative scientist," yet later says "However, any disinterested inquirer cannot fail to discover evidence of Nernst's arrogance and insensitivity toward the viewpoint of others. He was notoriously jealous concerning his priority, if not exclusivity, with regard to the discovery or enunciation of new scientific ideas, and he was repeatedly unwilling to give due credit to the work of others when it related to his own." The conspicuous lack of Nernst's support may help to explain Lewis's feelings.

The second area that many have felt was worthy of the award is the electron pair bond. When first proposed this was widely accepted and hailed by chemists, but physicists were reluctant to accept a view so deviant from the Bohr atom. The valence work was opposed or neglected by many physicists but a quotation from Heitler[238] shows that this was not a universal view: "Long before wave mechanics was known Lewis put forward a semi-empirical theory according to which the covalent bond between atoms was effected by the formation of pairs of electrons shared by each pair of atoms. We now know that wave mechanics affords a full justification of this picture, and, moreover, gives a precise meaning to these electron pairs: they are pairs of electrons with antiparallel spins." It is this area which many of today's chemists feel should have been the basis of the award. A possible reason that this did not lead to the prize is that there were only about four papers and the book, in the face of larger numbers of Langmuir's papers on related subjects. As a matter of interest, Langmuir, who was awarded the prize for entirely different work, was one of many who nominated Lewis for the prize.[201] For some reason, this contribution from Lewis that is used by every chemistry student to this day, was not considered worthy. Possibly the advances in quantum mechanics which ultimately supported the electron pair bond were not at the stage developed by Pauling and were therefore thought to show that the electron pair bond was no more than a useful counting device.

The third area, the isolation and study of heavy water and related deuterium compounds was a major technical achievement. He made deuterium compounds available to the scientific community. His determination of the properties of heavy water and other deuterium compounds on a minute scale was an experimental tour de force. The Nobel prize in 1934 was awarded to H. C. Urey (a former Lewis PhD) for the discovery of the heavy isotope of hydrogen at about the same time that Lewis' papers were coming out. Urey had shown that water electrolysis did concentrate deuterium, but this concentration was only to the extent of making it spectroscopically detectable. Lewis however did this on a large scale, allowing the preparation of significant and chemically useful amounts. Many have felt that a joint prize or a second prize would have been appropriate, but the timing was certainly difficult.

The work on acids and bases is frequently also cited as a possible basis of a Nobel Prize. In fact this area is the one more than any other remembered by more recent Nobel laureates as the most lasting, along with the electron pair bond. Letters to Harold Paretchan showing this point are quoted in part in a later chapter.

Keith Laidler, wrote a question in a historical article[239] asking why Lewis and Henry Eyring were not awarded the prize and offering several reasons why they both should have received it. Laidler presents his comments under the heading:

The Curious Incident of the Nobel Prizes.

"I call your attention to the Nobel prizes awarded to G. N. Lewis and Henry Eyring", as Sherlock Holmes might have said.

"But they were not awarded Nobel prizes."

"That was the curious incident," remarked Sherlock Holmes.

Laidler then goes on to document why these omissions were curious, summing up an argument based on the valence work which was opposed or neglected by many physicists with the exception of the above quotation from Heitler.

In this connection it may be noted that Henry Eyring, for whom Laidler also gives a convincing argument, was well known especially for his work on the theory of reaction rates. Eyring was a Berkeley PhD in 1928. He showed how reaction rates could be understood in terms of the thermodynamic properties of the "transition state," a concept which has proven useful up to the present time.

Jolly[201] presents a list of 34 nominations of Lewis for the Nobel prize covering the years 1922 to 1935, made by about twenty nominators, some of whom nominated more than once. There may have been later nominations as well.

It is of interest to note that he was a coauthor of ten papers with four Nobel prize winners (T. W. Richards, E. O. Lawrence, G. T. Seaborg and M. Calvin, all of whom received the award well after this coauthorship.) Their Nobel citations were not remotely related to any area of these collaborations. Seaborg[228] wrote "And, somehow, the Nobel Foundation made one of their rare mistakes by not awarding him the Nobel Prize in chemistry."

Although the Nobel prize eluded him, the list of honors awarded him is impressive. He was awarded honorary degrees from the University of Chicago, the University of Liverpool, the University of Pennsylvania, the University of Madrid and the University of Wisconsin (at the same ceremony in 1928 an honorary degree was also given to Charles A. Lindbergh). He won the Arrhenius Medal of the Royal Swedish Academy, the Davy Medal of the Royal Society of London, the Franklin Medal of the Franklin Institute, the Medal of the Society of Arts and Sciences, and the Nichols Medal, the Gibbs Medal, and the Richards Medal, all three administered by the American Chemical Society. He was a foreign member of the Danish Academy of Science, the Royal Society, the Royal Institute of Chemistry, the Indian Academy of Science, and the Academy of Sciences of the USSR. He was a member of the American Chemical Society, the American Physical Society, and the American Philosophical Society.

He was elected a member of the National Academy of Sciences in 1913. He resigned from the academy in 1934, after several years of being head of the chemistry section. The reasons for this were not clear, in fact a letter (in the Lewis archives in the Bancroft Library) from his old friend Gay chided Lewis, not for resigning, but for not making his reasons better known. Some of the reasons offered without evidence were the failure to elect his colleagues at an early enough stage (suggested names were Gibson, Giauque and Simon Freed). The idea that the eastern establishment did not take all of the west seriously was suggested, as was the idea that the organization was an "old boy" network, but no entirely satisfactory answer has surfaced. It may well have been a combination of all these factors, or Lewis may have been making a threat to which the academy did not respond. However, I have recently heard a possibly definitive story told to me by Mike Kasha, his last student. According to Kasha[240], who was Lewis' only coworker for this late period and therefore conversed with him on many subjects, Lewis had nominated Gibson for membership in the academy, but the recommendation was ignored, even though Lewis was head of the chemistry section of the academy. Lewis took this as a personal affront, and resigned.

Similarly, Jolly[201] notes that Lewis did offer his resignation as dean once at Berkeley, in protest to what he regarded as a salary injustice. The resignation as dean was not accepted. There is some parallel to the case of A. Krogh, himself a Nobel prize winner, who resigned from the Royal Danish Academy in 1949. He believed that the academy needed rejuvenating and hoped to prod them into it[241].

Chapter X   Lewis, Lachman, Conversation and Cards

The book[204] by Arthur Lachman, "Borderland of the Unknown, the Life Story of Gilbert Newton Lewis, One of the Worlds Greatest Scientists", is full of personal stories and reminiscences. It was written for a general reader, and therefore its value as a story of Lewis's science is purposely limited. The title is derived from the dedication of Lewis and Randall[77]: "Let this book be dedicated to chemists of the newer generation, who will not wish to reject all inference from conjecture or surmise, but who will not care to speculate concerning that which may be surely known. The fascination of a growing science lies in the work of the pioneers at the very borderland of the unknown, but to reach this frontier one must pass over well-traveled roads; of these one of the safest and surest is the broad highway of thermodynamics". It will be noticed that Lewis had strayed from the example of T. W. Richards, who did not approve of speculation, but instead waited until the question had a firm experimental answer. There are in Lewis' work many examples of "conjecture and surmise", often leading to fruitful lines of research.

Arthur Lachman was trained as an organic chemist in Germany. He was not a faculty member; he had had teaching positions elsewhere and had many years of experience in the chemical industry. At Berkeley, he was a research associate, a title without salary he held starting in 1920 and continuing after Lewis' death. He was very grateful to Lewis for giving him this opportunity. Except for substitute teaching for one year, he did not participate in the teaching, nor did he direct graduate students. He had a lab. on the main floor of the chemistry building while I was an undergraduate, and I would often see him working alone there. (Nowadays, of course, working alone in the lab. is considered very unsafe. It is surprising how many chemists of that era survived in the absence of these universal safety rules). I recall that he was working on the Beckmann rearrangement.

Lachman had worked in industry for several years, and (because he was unsalaried) could do consulting without penalty, as long as the department and the university were not mentioned in connection with this work. Soon after taking this unpaid position he contributed to an oil refining problem and became rather wealthy, making the unpaid job even more attractive. He initiated a fund used to help students and junior faculty which still existed many years later. His background made him much more tolerant of industrial chemistry than the regular faculty members were, and this attitude shows frequently in the book. The book is not a very valuable source of information about Lewis' chemistry, but it is a mass of anecdotes of a more personal nature, and it sheds some light on his character.

Lachman describes in some detail the dinners, held every month or so at The Fashion Restaurant, commonly known as The Fly Trap, a San Francisco Italian restaurant. Lachman calls these the "Dago dinners"; this now politically incorrect designation was not believed to be offensive then. In addition to food and wine, the major attraction was the conversation. The description of the food and drink need not concern us, except to note that when the Lewis family got old enough, an annual treat was a dinner in a good San Francisco restaurant. Lewis is described by Lachman as a witty and brilliant conversationalist, which contrasts sharply with his discomfort at speaking before large groups.

I wish that I could remember and reproduce the stories, jokes and puns that he would tell us. Only a few very bad puns remain and the merest outlines of the shaggy dog story, which described a man's lifelong search for his lost dog over the whole world, ending after a long time with a dog in Russia which was shown to him, and he sadly said "It's not shaggy enough". The many mother-in-law jokes that he collected for my grandmother are all forgotten. Lachman says that he composed many limericks, of which a few would come home with him.

Lunchtime at the faculty club was still another opportunity for sparkling conversation. Most colleagues of his era remember the lunch time at the faculty club even though Lewis did not always eat lunch. However, the period from noon to two was a social occasion, and he did participate with enthusiasm in the contract bridge games. He told me about the "Hearts" games, highly modified from the game played by children, and considered challenging even by the card experts at the club. In this connection, I was fascinated by Gerald Branch at the bridge table; he would pick up his hand in such a way that he could see all the cards, but he wouldn't sort them by suits or put them in any kind of order. This would have been a feat for most players, but it was commonplace for Branch, one of the best of the bridge players. I ultimately understood that this was a device to keep opponents from guessing about his hand, based upon the position that the card came from on every trick. Lewis was a spectator as well as a player at the chess games and the Kriegspiel games (this is a game using three chess boards, only the umpire can see more than one board, the players move silently and the umpire tells if the move is not possible, as one which is blocked by the presence of a piece he cannot see or one which puts the king in check; the umpire also announces captures and "check" or "mate"). I remember that in Inverness we constructed a Kriegspiel board out of a long piece of plywood with the three boards painted on. It only required sight barriers and three chess sets. My father lived in a room at the top floor of the faculty club while the family was in Inverness; he would have friends over for poker regularly. He had a great card sense and could pick up a new game rapidly, and both his sons learned to play all sorts of card games from him.

Lachman has numerous comments on Lewis as a kind and gentle man and gives several examples, one of which is finding a place for Lachman as "Research Associate", a position without salary, but with a laboratory and access to the chemistry storeroom, which allowed Lachman to do his own research in organic chemistry for many years. Another tale of his consideration for others concerned Axel Olson's hospital stay while a graduate student; Lewis would visit him every day until he was cured, perhaps not the usual behavior of a dean in a major university. Emphasis is also given to Lewis' social graces and humor in small groups, such as at the faculty club or the Dago dinners.

Lewis had a wide variety of friends, I did not know many of them but the names of some of them can be reconstructed. These included Jack Lowenberg, a professor of philosophy whose family we also knew well, Stephen Pepper (another philosopher), J. E. Tippett, whom I never met, Leonard Bacon, for many years a poet in the English department, but the friendship continued long after Bacon had left and gone east. Then there were William Bray, a respected colleague and friend going back to MIT days, Gerald Branch, one of his earliest graduate students and a colleague of enormous value, William Gay (I know about him because he had a son of almost exactly my age) had been on the Berkeley faculty but left to go to some kind of a medical school position in New York, Ernest Gibson, a colleague of long standing and a family friend, Walter Cannon, a Harvard friend who kept in touch for many years. Gerald Marsh was one of the card players. Harry Morse, another Harvard friend who was at Berkeley for only a brief time, was a family friend who was on the physics faculty at Stanford for years and whose family also came often to Inverness. Professor Ivan Linforth, a classicist, and his wife Kate were long time family friends. Membership in the drama section of the University brought in further friends to both Lewis and my mother; I remember only one of these, Prof. Goldsworthy, because I took a course in mathematics from him. Membership in the drama section cost Lewis a more than twenty year old mustache in the interest of simulating a play character. I remember how strange he looked for some time while it grew back.

Chapter XI   Lewis as Family Man

Before leaving Cambridge to go to California my father settled his future by getting married in 1912 to Mary Hinckley Sheldon, daughter of Edward Stevens Sheldon and Katherine Hinckley Sheldon; she was descended from a long line of Hinckleys going back at least to one who was colonial governor of the Plymouth colony. Sheldon was professor of romance philology at Harvard and was a well known etymologist (he was responsible for many of the derivations in the first edition of the Merriam-Webster unabridged dictionary). His family was from Maine and he was only one of several brothers who achieved distinction. I was named after him.

As far as I can tell, they went on a honeymoon to Tahiti before getting to Berkeley. One story from this honeymoon is that they were in an outrigger canoe when a very large wave turned it over and threw them into the ocean. From then on the versions of the story vary. According to my father he rescued my mother by seizing her very long hair, thus dragging her to safety. In the other version the story, Mary's hair was used to haul Gilbert to safety. Whatever the truth, they both survived and allowed the continuation of a distinguished scientific career and the establishment of this branch of the Lewis family in Berkeley.

The Lewis family started to grow; Richard Newton Lewis was born in 1916, his sister Margery was born in 1917 and I was born in 1920, well after the war. The peregrinations of the family started around this time, for I don't remember that the family ever owned a house in Berkeley. I remember at least seven different houses we rented in Berkeley. However, my sister believed that a house on Hillside Avenue was actually owned before 1923. Lewis was not a stupid man with respect to financial problems, for he left my mother a comfortable living, but certainly after 1923 he did avoid the classically recommended investment in a house in Berkeley. A major fire in 1924 burned a large, mostly residential, section of Berkeley north of the campus; this may have influenced his aversion to owning a house there.

In 1923, he did buy the house in Inverness that was home to the family during the summer and was initially used through the winters too. Inverness is a village in Marin County about forty miles north of San Francisco on the western shore of Tomales Bay. Unlike the eastern shore of the bay the western shore is heavily wooded with a variety of trees. It is separated from the ocean by a ridge, not quite large enough to screen out the roar of the surf when it is heavy, nor to keep the summer fog away completely.

The house was really unsuitable for winter living for it was uninsulated and the inadequate heating was from a fireplace, wood burning stoves and portable kerosene heaters. Thus later we came to live in rented houses in Berkeley during the winter and would move to Inverness for the summer while my father lived in the faculty club. He also purchased, perhaps in the late 1920s, a ramshackle house on quite a lot of land outside of Lafayette approachable only by crossing a rotting bridge; we never used the house. It was presumably bought as a land investment.

Inverness was founded by Scots, of whom only one remained to my memory. Tomales bay, is a long narrow salt water bay with a connection to the Pacific at the north end and represents a major part of the San Andreas fault in Marin County. It was thought to resemble Loch Ness in Scotland which is also a long narrow body of water with the original Inverness at the end. Tomales bay never had a monster, though. There used to be many signs of the 1906 earth quake on this fault, but few of them are still easy to find. Some are preserved on a trail near the entrance to the Point Reyes National Seashore Park.

The house in Inverness got a great deal of use in the early years, but Inverness was not as accessible as it is now. To get to it by car, one took the ferry from Richmond to Marin county, and then took various routes to get to Point Reyes Station and then drove over the dike at the end of Tomales bay to Inverness. This was not very fast, but it was reliable except when high water flooded the dike, and one could get from Berkeley to Inverness often in less than two hours. Now with the bridge and some much improved roads, it takes about forty minutes. To go by public transportation originally one took the electric train to the ferry to San Francisco, then another ferry to Sausalito, then a train from there to Manor. A narrow gauge train then went from Manor to Point Reyes Station, and if one was lucky, a sort of bus would go the last four miles to Inverness. We did this sometimes with baggage enough to last through the summer and the trip took most of the day. Even now public transportation still requires going by way of San Francisco, but a bus goes all the way from San Francisco to Inverness, sometimes more than once a day. The narrow gauge train has been abandoned, although most of the route is still easy to trace.

Lewis in the country: The Lewis family was mostly brought up in Inverness, together with initially short periods in Berkeley. G. N. Lewis spent more time in Berkeley than the rest of the family, but enjoyed the respite of Inverness often on week ends and sometimes for longer periods. Lewis is regarded widely as a highly civilized man, and in his career he was always in a metropolitan environment. Of course Berkeley was a rather small city, but even in the earlier days it was next to the larger city of Oakland and across the bay from San Francisco, which was easily reached by frequent ferry service. One sees later photographs almost invariably showing his usual gray suit with necktie, suggesting that he never dressed for the country. A sentence from Hildebrand (quoted by Stranges)[216],footnote 1, p188, contrasting Lewis and Langmuir, reads: "Lewis was an indoor man, an omnivorous reader, much given to reflection, a scientific philosopher". While this was doubtless an astute observation, it should be taken in the context of the contrast to the out-of-doors man Langmuir as written by the ultimate out-of-doors chemist Hildebrand, who was very active in the Sierra Club and was an avid skier.

Lewis did enjoy the outdoors to a significant extent. His son Richard[205] said that Gilbert Lewis had a love of nature possibly acquired when his father and family lived on the outskirts of Lincoln. There were trees, not common in Nebraska, near the house which attracted numerous birds. The rarity of trees in Nebraska is suggested by the name the "Tree Planters State" which lasted until it became the "Cornhusker State". He was also a member of the Bohemian Club of San Francisco and spent some time in the associated Bohemian Grove, a camp in the redwoods on the Russian River. We had in Inverness a painting of this camp done by a fellow member showing the redwoods and some of the campers. This camp, I have since gathered, is not exactly primitive but at least it is outdoors.

The children all learned the local flora and fauna; my mother even became a mushroom expert, to the extent that we enjoyed eating a variety of the local wild mushrooms. Apparently her expertise was sufficient, for we never suffered any ill effects.

In Inverness he enjoyed getting out to the ocean or some of the more distant beaches on Tomales bay. It is true that he was not given to long hikes, backpacking, or other approaches to primitive areas, but he enjoyed greatly the places the could be reached by car and a modest hike. It was from him that I learned that crowds could be avoided by walking only a mile from automobile access. This is almost still true, except in the most popular national parks.

We went several times to the redwoods in the summer time, driving up to near Scotia and camping near the Van Duzen river but not very far from the car. There was also an earlier camping trip without me in the redwoods at Bull Creek, a tributary of the Russian River. In our camp we had a tent and cots, but my brother and sister and I would sleep in sleeping bags under the trees. We did not have all the food needed for an extended stay, instead we would drive into Scotia to get perishables. This form of camping is remote from the kind requiring carrying everything needed on back packs and is limited to California or other places where summer rain does not occur. My father did not wear his gray suit when camping.

My father did much of the camp cooking, showing us that it was quite practical to cook over an open fire. To get to the river for swimming and for water we had to walk dressed for swimming through the flood plain of the river overgrown with assorted shrubbery including mostly poison oak. I do not know to this day why no one of us ever came down with this poisoning; we were not immune for we all got it at one time or another in other locations. The drinking water did not come from the river, but from a minuscule waterfall on the other side of the river which required a swim of about ten feet in the summer. Presumably in the rainy season there was far more water in this small river since the flood plain was more than 50 ft. wide and was strewn with rounded boulders that spoke of long and turbulent trips down the winter river at some earlier time. There was dead grass caught up on the poison oak, a relic of very recent winter flooding. Only on rare occasions would we see a stranger near our camp. The redwoods, although quite large, were apparently mostly second growth left from very early lumbering operations. A redwood tree can get quite large in fifty years; we had one in Inverness growing in an unfavorable location, but it is still about three feet across at the base.

On another occasion we took a canoe on the car to an approach to Abbott's lagoon (off the ocean near Inverness, now in the Point Reyes National Seashore Park), loaded up the canoe and paddled it across the lagoon to the east end of a big sand dune and camped there for several days (in those days the lagoon was deeper and was free from dams; it was good for swimming although the water was brackish). I remember waking up early in the morning there seeing a deer staring at us through the fog.

The ocean beach, a twelve mile long strip of wide beach between Point Reyes and Tomales point (now mostly in the Point Reyes National Seashore Park), held a fascination for my father, he would seek a part of it where other people were out of sight if not wholly absent; we could walk along the beach for hours without seeing anyone. The beach was well supplied with driftwood allowing cooking over the open fire. Now the use of the beach by many more people coupled with the lessening in the number of lumber rafts offshore have made the driftwood less plentiful; furthermore the National Park Service does not allow open fires.

Post-war and later: The period immediately after the war was partly characterized by prohibition, a law instituted during the war. After the repeal my father and my mother would often have a drink before dinner. But even before the repeal there was the age of cocktails, and my father like most others at this time had a recipe of his own which I suppose I was too young to know about. There clearly was a friendly and prosperous bootlegger who kept my father supplied: The ocean beach was used by other bootleggers to bring in spirits; the cost of the boat which was wrecked nearly every time was more than covered by the high prices that the cargo drew. In Inverness one could take a gallon jug to one of the Italian families in the neighborhood (again I didn't know which of the many such families in Inverness) and get it filled with the homemade red wine from the barrel for an exceedingly modest price. I do remember a large party in celebration of repeal and the defeat of those terrible Republicans by the election of Franklin Roosevelt. However, eight or ten years later Lewis thought that Roosevelt was awful. In fact, I cannot characterize his political views, except to guess that, like the rest of his character, they were very individualistic. Although he had strong opinions, he was not politically active, he had an Al Smith campaign button in 1928; this was as far as I know the limit of his political activism.

The Lewis Household: Some details of the household are relevant to the family life. In addition to my father, my mother, my sister and my brother, there were at times others. My father's mother, Mary Burr Lewis, lived with us for a period near the end of her life. I do not remember much about her, but I think now she would have been diagnosed as having Alzheimer's disease; she did not to my recollection tell stories about my father when he was young. She died in the late twenties. We did not learn where her middle name came from even if later we guessed (apparently incorrectly) that it might have been from the rather infamous Aaron. My maternal grandmother and her husband lived with us for a while. I remember my grandfather Sheldon only vaguely as a short, bearded man; I don't remember that he stayed with us very long. The short stature came to me and my brother and sister then from both sides of the family. My grandmother Sheldon lived alone in Berkeley for many years after her husband died, although we of course saw her often. She did spend the last few months of her life with us. She was the butt of the numerous mother-in-law jokes that my father used to collect. My father must have been quite prosperous by the standards of chemistry professors now, since we had in residence for many years two employees. The first was a cook from Yorkshire, Miss Hanson, who passed on to my mother her valued technique for roast beef and Yorkshire pudding. The second was a sort of nanny and tutor, Susan van Zandt (we called her Vanny), who had once been a teacher. She was entrusted with much of the care of the children and some of our early education.

We were read to by my mother, who would sometimes do whole books in nightly installments; I recall her reading *The Hound of the Baskervilles* with one night's reading ending "Mr. Holmes, it was the footprint of a gigantic hound." Needless to say, we were ready to hear more the next night. Reading at night in Inverness was at first not easy, for there was no electricity, and only one kerosene lamp really gave enough light to read by. I remember being told that reading by one of the feebler lamps would ruin my eyes, but this did not seem to happen. We did get electricity in Inverness about as soon as it became available there, the house was wired by my father and Dick. I was entrusted to do only one simple job which immediately resulted in a blown fuse, which was instructive if not helpful.

Education: We three children were given a rather unusual education, reminiscent of Gilbert's own education. Schools were avoided up to the high school level. The example of my father and his sister were followed closely. Two quotations are relevant in this context. One found by Hildebrand[203], is that Lewis attributed his own advantage to having "escaped some of the ordinary processes of formal education." Again, my mother gave Lachman[204] a memorandum she found from G. N. Lewis: "It doesn't take so much intelligence to get along, if you haven't been to school." This theme of avoiding the school system was clear to all of us and we didn't miss it much except that Margery was a more social creature than her two brothers and chafed at the isolation before she finally did go to school.

In Inverness we studied with my mother and Vanny. All three of us studied French with Mrs. Logan, who lived nearby. The Logan family was on our party line in a telephone system that was primarily intended to allow communication with the ranches. It was not part of the Bell system but in emergencies it could connect to it, allowing long distance calls to Berkeley. Mrs. Logan was Irish and had been raised in a French convent, as a consequence my later use of French in France had a rather stilted and old-fashioned vocabulary; I was not good at the slang. She also was my first violin teacher. In Berkeley we all studied German with chemistry graduate students or post-docs from Germany. To my later regret as a Texas resident, Spanish was not considered necessary for a good education.

On weekends and in Berkeley, my father would give us exercises in arithmetic and would propound various puzzles, and we would play word games of various kinds. I remember learning geography from large maps of Europe, Asia, Africa, and North and South America posted in our Inverness rooms. I still remember two rivers starting with X that were useful when the person ahead in a geography game would come up with Essex, requiring a geographical reply starting with X. In Inverness, studies were never forgotten and in addition to French, music, arithmetic, etc., we also studied birds and flowers using standard reference books. I still have a notebook showing my drawings of the various birds. I think this was the limit of my art training, certainly I can't draw any better now than these primitive and rough pictures of an eight year old without artistic talent.

In Berkeley, we studied solfege privately with Margaret Prall, who taught at Mills College. I continued violin with her, Margery studied piano with my mother, who was an accomplished pianist, and both Margery and Dick took voice lessons. The gut E string which had frustrated my father was no longer a problem, since the wire E string came in before I started, so I continued to study with Louis Ford in San Francisco until after I was in the University, and I still play. If I inherited science from my father, I inherited music from my mother. Only many years later did I realize how talented a pianist my mother was. Except for Dick's few weeks in a Swiss boarding school, we successfully stayed away from schools for years.

Finally, Dick left for school, he enrolled in The Deep Springs School, an institution in the southern California desert of very high reputation which combined a boarding school with a working farm. He stayed there for about two mostly enjoyable years, earning college level credits before coming back to Berkeley. He then enrolled in the University, where he majored in chemistry, but in the College of Letters and Science rather than in the College of Chemistry.

My sister Margery was next to leave for school; she went to the Dominican Convent in San Rafael, where she had a miserable time. The Dominican convent had an excellent academic reputation as a boarding school. She tells me that she had wanted to go away to a boarding school, and this was considered the best nearby. It was, however, a great disappointment to her; she felt like a prisoner. We went up to visit on weekends in the winter and would eat a picnic lunch by the roadside where my mother would read to us stories about Aristide Pujol[236] for a while before returning Margery to her virtual prison. She only stayed there for a year before being released to go to Anna Head's school in Berkeley, where she had friends. The idea of sending children away from home to school might have been suggested to my father by the system in high class British families, but I think that it might have been instead a comment on the nearby schools, together with his own unusual educational experience. Certainly both Deep Springs and Anna Head's were regarded as superior schools, and certainly the neighborhood public schools had no such reputation. Margery followed her mother's example who had studied for about two years at Radcliffe, with about two years at U. C.

When it came my turn to go to high school, my parents selected the A-to-Zed school. It was within walking distance of home in Berkeley; it was a rather strange private school that no longer exists. There were some wonderful t eachers, there were several university faculty children there, but there was also a considerable contingent of "students" who had been thrown out of other schools for both academic and disciplinary reasons and it was for many of these a last resort. I did have some of the good teachers (as well as a chemistry teacher who was fifty years behind the times) and did well enough to be admitted to Berkeley and the College of Chemistry at an early age.

My brother Dick graduated from Berkeley three years ahead of me, in 1937. Dick spent a year in Oxford at Brasenose College before returning to Cal Tech for a PhD with Carl Nieman. He then joined the General Electric Company in Schenectady, and his career was in the chemical industry until his retirement except for about a year or so with the University of Delaware.

I went to Harvard for graduate work and got my PhD with Paul D. Bartlett in 1947; my graduate studies were interrupted by two years in the Navy, nearly all of which was after the war was over. After the PhD, I spent a year at UCLA and associated myself with Saul Winstein before coming permanently to Rice.

The question of why Margery was sent to the Dominican Convent to some might suggest that the Roman Catholic religious training was part of the arrangement. This would have been far from the truth, religion was not a part of my parents life, and they saw no reason to include it in their chidren's lives either. I find it hard to find any trace of religious training in either parent. A suggestion from my sister that the Frank Lewis family members were Presbyterians may be true, but there is little evidence that it had much influence on them or my father. It was said that one of my mother's grandparents was a Unitarian, but there is no record, and many would claim that that is not a religion anyway. My father was very well read and presumably had read the Bible at some stage, he was familiar with biblical stories of one kind or another, but certainly gave us no evidence that he regarded them as more than history or fiction. The family when we were together was essentially areligious rather than antireligious or religious. It is often assumed that religion is necessary to provide a moral and ethical background, yet my parents were both highly moral and ethical, and I have not seen those qualities lacking in my siblings either.

Home schooling nowadays often has the connotation of special religious training, not obtainable in the public schools by virtue of the separation of church and state doctrine. Clearly this was not in the minds of my parents; they believed that learning at home was simply a much better way to learn a great deal more, I still believe it to be true although I did not apply it to my own family.

Both my brother and I had careers in chemistry, and the question of whether our father pressured us into this will occur. I can only speak for myself and can assert that I never felt any pressure or even suggestion that I should go into this field. Before entering college, I was sure that some area of science was what I wanted, probably either chemistry or physics. Perhaps the choice of chemistry was merely the least trouble. However, the early education did certainly develop in me thought processes that were to some extent shaped by my father's own fascination with science. I can not say whether my own interest in science was inherited, but I am sure that my education was a very important factor.

My brother Dick's course was not that different from mine and I never got the feeling that he regretted going all the way to the PhD in chemistry. After his PhD he went into the chemical industry, but his interest in science remained strong even after retirement. In his last years (he died in 1991) since his retirement to Inverness he developed a new interest in cosmology. This led to some as yet unpublished ideas on an alternative to the "big bang" which have to some extent been taken over by his son, also G. N. Lewis (hereafter called "Gil), who is a mathematics professor at Michigan Tech. This rather reminded me of my father attacking conventional American anthropology in his last years.

My sister Margery never had any interest in science, and appears to have resisted both the effects of heredity and education. When I was an undergraduate there were girls who were chemistry majors, so there was no really great obstacle to studying science had she had the interest. She did have an active social life.

At home when my father was there he taught us numerous card games, since he was himself an addict. There were various word games during weekend dinners. These included the "Geography Game" in which in turn one had to find the name of a geographical unit starting with the same letter as the previous players unit's last letter. It would become more difficult if the preceding player would specify the kind of unit, as city or river. When traveling by car we would play a game called roadside cribbage, in which a dog on a roof or a cat in a window would count many more points than the same animal on the ground. Being the first to spot a license plate of an out of state car also was entertainment while driving.

Part of our education was the exposure to distinguished men at various times, a few of these I remember. When I was a small boy in Inverness, my father woke me up in the late evening and introduced me to Prof. Niels Bohr, saying that I would probably be grateful later for having met him. We met Linus Pauling on numerous occasions, since he spent several summers at Berkeley. Prof. Joffe from the USSR Academy came to Inverness once and had a picnic with us at the ocean.

Later in Berkeley Prof. L. Michaelis visited us at home for a meal; in addition to his chemistry he was a wonderfully talented pianist and musician. He could improvise in the style of almost any well known composer. I remember this better because in graduate school I gave a seminar talk on semiquinones, an area mostly developed by Michaelis in the late thirties. These visits were only incidental to the visits to the department; I did of course meet only a small fraction of department visitors.

Lewis and Inverness: During the summer when the family was up at Inverness, he had a room at the top floor of the faculty club where he would stay during the week. He would drive to Inverness on the weekends. Before he got a 1932 Dodge he would drive his 1924 Chrysler touring car which we could hear laboring up the hill nearly a half mile away to get to our house. His first car was a model T which I don't remember. Automobiles in those days had characteristic transmission noises, so it was no great feat to tell his car from others taking the same route. If we failed to spot the Chrysler noise, the dog would always react to it. This same car took us to the ocean beaches on these weekends. On one occasion I was told that we carried 14 people and a red setter out to the beach in it (before the days of a seat belt per person). These trips usually brought sand into the car, which got into the lock at the bottom of the gear shift lever so that we were not able to lock the car for years. Fortunately there were other switches which allowed the ignition to be shut off. The car was stolen more than once, but was hard enough to drive to prevent anyone from wanting to keep it. It had a running board that we liked to ride in Inverness without great hazard because neither the car nor the roads would allow fast driving, but on one occasion when the car was newer, my father claimed he had driven for a short stretch at 70. Lachman[204] claims that Lewis was habitually a fast and erratic driver; I had no one to compare him with but we all survived without problems. When the Chrysler became too unreliable, Dad acquired a 1935 Dodge, which he kept to the end.

My mother did not learn to drive until the 1930s and none of the kids drove until we were late teenagers. Curiously, although the ocean was less than five miles away, I do not remember ever walking to it. We did walk very often on weekday afternoons to Shell beach on Tomales Bay, but my father would not go there; there were too many people there on the crowded weekends; he preferred not being able to see anyone within miles. Because my mother had no car and didn't drive in most of this period we didn't go out to the ocean except when my father was in Inverness. We spent a few early winters in Inverness; this experience in a thin-walled house as free from heating as ours was a cold and wet ordeal. Inverness could have delightful weather at any time of the year, but it also could get quite cold, and the rainy season usually goes from the middle of November to March. When Dick and Margery went to school and when I finally went to school, the time in Inverness was greatly shortened.

Inverness was not a complete antithesis of Berkeley, there were reminders frequently. Several UC families had houses there or would rent houses in the summer. The family we knew best was the Gibsons. Ernest Gibson was one of the two earliest new colleagues of my father in the department, he had two sons and a daughter, of about the same age as the Lewis children. We collaborated by building a telegraph, between the two houses, based on an abandoned telephone line allowing communication (not everyone had a telephone) to arrange trips to Shell Beach on the bay or like endeavors. I still remember Morse code. On one occasion near the close of this period of summers in Inverness I sat on the Gibson's porch listening to Professor Gibson read his latest translations from Sanscrit, an occupation he developed late in life. Gibson, alone among American chemists, was the professor who had two graduate students who later won Nobel prizes. Another family often in Inverness was the Edward Tolman family, they had two girls and a boy. Edward Tolman was a professor of psychology and was the brother of Richard Tolman, one of the MIT chemists who had come to Berkeley with Lewis. Rudolph Schevill was on the Berkeley faculty in German, his two sons were Inverness regulars. There was a good deal of intermarriage among these summer residents, although neither my brother nor I married Inverness girls. We were charter members of the tennis club, but not the Yacht club. For some reason we never owned a sail boat and participated in sailing only in someone else's boat. We did have a canvas canoe which we could paddle up the bay although it was quite sensitive to the wind, a common summer weather feature. This canoe, still in use in the bay, is now about the only relic of the Lewis family existence in Inverness. The house is still there but has gone through several hands since who have made many internal changes. There were also permanent residents of Inverness; there were many Italian families, a few Scots left over from those who named the town, some native Americans, fishermen, and a town drunk, among others. My father was, I guess, rather careful (not to say snobbish) about our associations and there were Inverness residents with whom we did not mix. Some residents commuted to a radio communications station out closer to the ocean. Now, of course, there are even those who commute to San Francisco, since that trip is much faster.

Gilbert and Mary Lewis had three children, Richard Newton (Dick), Margery, and Edward Sheldon (Ted). All of these had children and all met together with his grandchildren and even one greatgreatgrandson at a family reunion in Inverness in

1986, while Mary Lewis, who was 95 at the time, was still living. However, only one of the grandchildren ever met their grandfather; Margery's daughter Sylvia (now Alcon) has a remote memory of her grandfather Lewis, whom she called Grandy. On one occasion she says that he entertained her with some tricks with napkins at the dinner table and once he showed her how to tie a shoe while sitting next to her on the steps. Since she was no more than three at the time these memories are obviously vague. Dick's son Jerry was born before G. N.'s death, but they lived at the time in Schenectady and as far as I know did not make it out to California in time. Margery's son David, Dick's other three children Gilbert Newton ("Gil"), Cynthia and Arthur, and my two sons Richard and Gregory were not born before his death. My father did meet Dick's wife, Helen, and Margery's husband, Jack Selby, but not my wife, Fofo.

Lewis' Health: In his later life he used to find a secluded spot in the dunes at the ocean beach and bask in the sun. I have since wondered if this was an early symptom of a loss of energy related to the heart trouble which later killed him. Of course he was over sixty when I remember him best, so the fact that I never saw him play tennis or golf, in both of which he had indulged as a younger man, might have only reflected his advancing years.

Only once did I see him ill and in bed. He had an infection diagnosed as erysipelas which a dozen or so years later would probably have succumbed rapidly to penicillin, it took weeks for him to recover. I did see a decline in his vigor for several years and find the final diagnosis of a fatal heart attack highly credible. In 1946 I was away when he died and did not see him after December of 1945, so I have no information on the state of his health in the intervening two months. The suggestion of suicide by cyanide in Jolly's book[201] (although originated earlier by Hildebrand and Pitzer, both of whom knew him well) is to me out of character, and not supported by the autopsy. He was still excited about his last two unpublished papers on the antiquity of American civilization and on glaciation when I last saw him.

His general health seemed as good as could be expected for a chain smoker of cigars. His diet would horrify cholesterol-conscious people now. When home, he would have scrambled eggs every morning for breakfast as well as oatmeal and cream and buttered toast. When he brought food to Inverness on a weekend in the summer it often would include a monstrous T-bone steak nearly two inches thick which we demolished before Monday. I have since wondered how my mother (or in earlier years the cook from Yorkshire) could cook this on our rather feeble kerosene stove, but I remember that it was delicious. While he lived at the faculty club I understand that he did not eat breakfast, so perhaps this excess was only a weekend thing, but in later years when my mother stayed in Berkeley through the summer and all three children were gone the breakfast was a daily feast. He did not then usually eat lunch at the faculty club, but still went there for contact with his friends and the bridge and chess.

Traveling: The spring semester of 1923 before we had the Inverness house, Lewis took his family to England for a sabbatical leave at Oxford; this was only the second time he had absented himself from Berkeley for any length of time. For this half year, C. W. Porter was acting dean and chairman. Of course he was away for a period during the first war. Thus from 1912 to 1941, my father was chairman and dean for all but something less than two years. Considering that his two major books came out in 1923, it is easy to see how a sabbatical leave would have been welcome. My brother and sister had good recollections of that trip. Margery remembered the house in Oxford and has a recollection of a trip to St. Jean de Luz in France and an image of very large pond with children sailing boats across it somewhere in France. From my own rather more recent experience, I surmise that this may have been the Luxembourg Gardens in Paris. I remember nothing about that trip, not surprising since I was just three.

We traveled to our camp in the redwoods in the Chrysler. There were places on the highway where it was actually possible to go at fifty miles per hour, to the delight of the kids. There was also the Cloverdale Hill which would cause the car to overheat, so we spent some travel time by the side of the road part way up the hill waiting for the engine to cool. Our camping place was a very long one day drive so we sometimes stopped for the night in a hotel along the way or back. We children looked forward to this, but Dad didn't. Perhaps in retrospect it was rather expensive. He did all the driving, since no one else in the family knew how or was old enough to drive. These trips became rarer as time went on.

I remember two long drives without camping. The first was to Deep Springs School; Dad, Margery, and I went down one spring to see my brother Dick. The wild flowers on the way were gorgeous, and the transition from Berkeley in the spring to the central valley and then the near desert was my first experience of the enormous variety of California scenery. I don't know exactly how long Dick stayed at Deep Springs, I doubt it was much longer than two years.

The other trip was later when my mother, my father and I went north as far as Crater Lake. I have not forgotten a magnificent view of Mt. Shasta on the way; I took a picture of it with the 4x5 camera my father gave me that he had brought back from the Phillipines nearly thirty years before. I used this camera for several years using film packs; this was easier than the glass plates he used. Trying to get the right exposure when the iris diaphragm was not calibrated in f numbers was a challenge; I am not surprised the my father did not bring back photographs from the Phillipines. We also spent a couple of weeks one summer in a rented house on Fallen Leaf Lake, near Lake Tahoe. I think there were some trips to the Sierras that only my mother and father took for brief vacations, perhaps only weekends. I only remember sketchy conversational references to Tahoe Meadows and to Grass Valley.

My father of course did quite a lot of traveling without taking the family. Destinations after the first war included Sweden, Spain, USSR, Ithaca, Ann Arbor, Chicago, Philadelphia and others that I have forgotten. Apparently the only southern hemisphere trip was that to Tahiti, mentioned earlier.

My father was accompanied on the USSR trip by my mother, and my brother was with them as far as Switzerland. There he was put in a boarding school until our parents returned from the Russian trip. That trip was in the company of scientists from everywhere; most of it consisted of a boat trip down the Volga with scientific meetings aboard the river boat. I had a brief correspondence with a Dr. Herbert Sachse, who at the time was the youngest delegate. He said believed he was the only survivor in 1982 of that 1928 Volga cruise, but he was mistaken since my mother lived for another five years after his letter. He was included among the highly distinguished group of scientists because he could speak Russian, as realized by Peter Debye, one of the other distinguished scientists. My parents enjoyed the company of the Charles Darwins; it now seems a long time ago but Darwin was not the famous Darwin; he was in fact the grandson of his more famous namesake. I don't know how much they were allowed ashore, but at the end of the boat trip they did get on land and went to Georgia before coming home via Moscow. I got a magnificent galena crystal from the Caucasus as a memento of that trip. The return from Moscow to the west by rail through Minsk is briefly described by Lachman[204]. First they attempted to cross the border into Poland but were rejected there, due to missing passport stamps which should have been done in Moscow. They were therefore sent back to Minsk. They were then fortunately rescued by a man who spoke German and a helpful Polish consul, thereby limiting their stay in an unspeakably bad Minsk hotel to only one horrid night. The children heard of this harrowing experience of the trip during which Lewis was made a foreign member of the Soviet academy.

Chapter XII   The Las Vegas Symposium

A symposium had been organized for an ACS meeting in December of 1946 to celebrate Lewis' accomplishments but his death forced a cancellation. In 1981 Derek Davenport organized a symposium, "Gilbert Newton Lewis 1875-1946." It was held at the spring 1982 ACS national meeting at Las Vegas. The papers were presented by many of his colleagues, former students, and others.

The papers at that meeting were later published in *J. Chem. Ed.* in the first three issues of 1984 as follows:

Richard N. Lewis[205] "A Pioneer Spirit from a Pioneer Family".

John Servos[209] "G. N. Lewis: The Disciplinary Setting."

Melvin Calvin and Glenn T. Seaborg[210] "The College of Chemistry in the G. N. Lewis Era: 1912-1946".

Melvin Calvin "Gilbert Newton Lewis: His Influence on Physical-Organic Chemists at Berkeley".[219]

Glenn T. Seaborg[222] "The Research Style of G. N. Lewis: Acids and Bases".

Leo Brewer[224] "The Generalized Lewis-Acid-Base Theory: Surprising Recent Developments".

Kenneth S. Pitzer[213] "Gilbert N. Lewis and the Thermodynamics of Strong Electrolytes".

Jacob Bigeleisen[220] "Gilbert N. Lewis and the Beginnings of Isotope Chemistry".

Anthony N. Stranges[216] "Reflections on the Electron Theory of the Chemical Bond".

Linus Pauling[217] "G. N. Lewis and the Chemical Bond".

William B. Jensen[214] "Abegg, Lewis, Langmuir, and the Octet Rule".

Michael Kasha[225] "The Triplet State: an Example of G. N. Lewis' Research Style".

Of these contributors two were G. N. Lewis PhD students (Bigeleisen and Kasha), four were Berkeley faculty (Brewer, Calvin, Pitzer and Seaborg), three were historians (Jensen, Servos and Stranges), Linus Pauling was a long time friend and scientific associate and Richard Lewis was the elder son.

This well attended symposium is not here reported in detail but is a source of the information used throughout this biography. It was one which I did not attend owing to a sudden faint occurring only minutes before the start which kept me hospitalized in Las Vegas for the whole week. I have assumed that the written reports closely followed the oral presentations. It will be noted that major parts of this text are based on the reports of this symposium.

CHAPTER XIII   Lewis as a Person

At this point the various pieces can be put together to present a picture of Lewis as a man. Someone not as close as I could perhaps do a better job on this area than I. He was to me a father, and I thought for a long time that he was what all fathers were. Only when I was older did I begin to see that he was an extraordinary man. We can describe him first physically, then go on in more detail in other characteristics.

My father when young had almost black hair, although it was gray for most of my recollection, with dark eyes. He wore a severe pointed black beard from some time in his MIT years until the start of his military service, and a moustache thereafter. He was a short man, apparently a family trait, continued in my generation, for my brother and sister and I were all rather short.

I do not remember him as a particularly athletic man, but he told the story of some kind of physical examination on entrance into Harvard where he was asked to do some pushups on the parallel bars; the examiner was distracted for a while at the end of which the pushups were continuing. I remember vaguely a time out at the ocean beach when we were playing some kind of game and I saw him run quite fast. The fact that I remember it suggests that it was a rare occurrence. In his youth he did play tennis and golf; as evidence our basement contained some ancient wood-shafted golf clubs. There are reports that he hiked extensively in the Phillipines during his stay there. At the ocean we would often walk a mile or so to avoid the crowds (crowds by my fathers standards would have been one or two people within a half mile), but I do not recall any very long hikes. However, walking a mile on sand is equivalent to much greater distances on a firm surface.

He usually wore a gray flannel suit with a necktie, even when away from the University, and occasionally a felt hat and overcoat in the winter. Photographs in the laboratory showed that he often did experiments with the whole suit on, but sometimes dispensed with the jacket. Modern chemists would be shocked not only at the lack of a lab coat, but also of eye protection. In later years he was somewhat, but not grossly, overweight. As a youth I believe he was quite slight. He wore glasses only for reading, and not always then. He was not in any sense a natty man, and often looked rather rumpled. The jacket pocket always held a few hours supply of cigars. This, together with a few photographs, gives some idea of his general appearance.

Lewis did not enjoy speaking in public, although he did on several occasions. He gave no regular lectures at Berkeley, he seldom presented papers at scientific meetings or even attended these except for a few special invited lectures. The Silliman Lectures at Yale were one such as was the lecture at the Franklin Institute, and there is also a record of at least one lecture before the University, and one at UCLA. The Franklin Lecture in Philadelphia was given with lecture demonstrations of the color changes of indicators. These few examples over a period of dozens of years illustrate the rarity of these presentations, and helps to establish his reluctance to speak in public. Yet in small groups of friends he was a willing and entertaining contributor to the general talk. On social occasions he was a brilliant conversationalist, and had an unlimited supply of jokes and stories. He would also contribute pithy and humorous *bon mots* to the conversation. He had a supply of limericks, some even suitable for mixed company. He was also addicted to puns, an affliction which he passed on to both his sons.

His reluctance to speak formally in public did not extend to the written word. He was a master of this form of expression. The most widely quoted of example of his fluency with words is the preface to the book "Thermodynamics and the Free Energy of Chemical Substances" by Lewis and Randall[77]. Only part of this is quoted here:

"There are ancient cathedrals which, apart from their consecrated purpose, inspire solemnity and awe. Even the curious visitor speaks of serious things, with hushed voice, and as each whisper reverberates through the vaulted nave, the returning echo seems to bear a message of mystery. The labor of generations of architects and artisans has been forgotten, the scaffolding erected for their toil has long since been removed, their mistakes have been erased, or have been hidden by the dust of centuries. Seeing only the perfection of the completed whole, we are impressed as by some superhuman agency. But sometimes we enter such an edifice that is still partly under construction; then the sound of hammers, the reek of tobacco, the trivial jests bandied from workman to workman, enable us to realize that these great structures are but the result of giving to ordinary human effort a direction and a purpose.

"Science has its cathedrals, built by the efforts of a few architects and of many workers. In these loftier monuments of scientific thought a tradition has arisen whereby the friendly usages of colloquial speech give way to a certain severity and formality. While this may sometimes promote precise thinking, it more often results in the intimidation of the neophyte. Therefore we have attempted, while conducting the reader through the classic edifice of thermodynamics into the workshops where construction is now in progress, to temper the customary severity of the science in so far as is compatible with clarity of thought......"

This is the most celebrated example of his writing style, but many others worthy of quotation to show his writing skill could be found, some in highly technical passages, others intended for the layman.

Lewis was generally a genial and polite man. He, however, did not tolerate stupidity or badly thought out ideas. In his position as administrator he was strong and ready to try out new ideas, especially his own. He was in many ways almost dictatorial, but did allow change when the first try failed He was a fount of knowledge on almost any subject; I learned a great deal from him outside of the educational process, even though that was going on most of the time. He was very tolerant of me and the family; I do not remember ever seeing him angry, although disapproval was clear when called for. He made no secret of his opinions, and we learned to pay attention to these, even when our inclinations were opposite. He liked good food and drink, although I never recognized that he was even faintly drunk.

His music taste was developed rather early; he told me that he had briefly studied the violin but gave it up partly because the gut E strings were constantly breaking. His favorite composers were almost all of the 18th and 19th centuries, and he had little tolerance for atonality and other modern discordant compositions. He used to liken some of these to a visit to the dentist who would search around for a sensitive spot and drill there, just as the composer would seek for some especially onerous dissonance and persistently repeat it.

His taste in art escaped me, except one year at our Christmas time charade party his choice of our title to illustrate was the DuChamps painting then in the public eye: "Nude Descending the Stairs". I remember these charades as places for outrageous puns with some of the most extreme committed by the Ernest Gibson family. George Adams was a family friend and professor of philosophy who also participated with his family in these annual charade parties, as did Steven Pepper, another philosophy professor, and his family. Professor Loewenberg and his wife and daughter also participated often.

He enjoyed games and other diversions, but always demanded some intellectual challenge. Indeed, exercising his intellect was constant. It was his profession, it was also his relaxation. He did not have major hobbies (except card games and the like) but he never liked automatic or senseless occupations. His major interest was science, especially chemistry. I can not understand the life he led with hours spent in the laboratory even when his family was enjoying Inverness in the summer without the realization that he loved chemistry more than anything else. He spent many hours in the lab. including weekends and evenings even during the times we were all in Berkeley.   I sometimes wonder how my mother survivedthis neglect.

Lewis was never given to any conspicuous show of affection, my family knew that he was very fond of us, but the evidence of this to outsiders was sparse. Perhaps he showed most affection to his daughter, Margery. He always showed us all respect, however. He was a kindly man and I remember no scenes of dispute or rancour.

There were family pets but I don't remember that he ever played with them. I have a memory of him sitting with the large orange cat, Tigger, on his lap and stroking it.

He had an individualistic approach to problems. He was once asked whether, in adding up a column of figures he went from top to bottom or the reverse. His reply was that he did it both ways and took the average. This presumably jocular answer displays the fact that he did not like senseless rules; they did not confine him. Kasha[225] commented on his technique of attacking a problem which would often yield only after going both ways from the beginning and from the end.

Chapter XIV Paretchan and the Letters to him

This biography cannot be completed without reference to the efforts of Harold Paretchan, a resident of Weymouth, MA. Harold Paretchan is not a scientist, his major avocation up to the point of discovering Lewis was the compilation of baseball statistics. Mr. Paretchan learned a few years ago that Weymouth was the birthplace of Gilbert Newton Lewis, who turned out to have been a very distinguished chemist, although no one in Weymouth knew anything about him or his local connection. Mr. Paretchan, set about to correct this in an extraordinary display of zeal and persistence. This effort may be divided into two sections, although they are inextricably connected. The first are the efforts to get recognition in Weymouth, in Massachusetts and in the whole country. The second is a massive correspondence with distinguished scientists, mostly Nobel prize winners, around the world to give credence to non-scientists to the thesis that Lewis was in reality a man of immense distinction worthy of all these efforts. This correspondence has very recently been extended to department chairmen of an increasing number of major universities excerpts from which I have not been able to include. This biography would probably never have been started without Paretchan's efforts.

In Weymouth, Mr. Paretchan worked on the town government and the Board of Selectmen to have the street on which the Lewis family lived named in his honor. Unfortunately, this is a major street in the town, Commercial Street. Thus the number of addresses that would have had to be changed was large, so the request was turned down. Paretchan's efforts have not ceased; a street named G. N. Lewis has now been promised and he is still working on a plaque at the location of the Lewis house. He succeeded in having a Gilbert Newton Lewis Recognition Day declared in the town.

A recent local triumph was the dedication of the science area in the local high school as the Gilbert Newton Lewis Science area, and this dedication was attended by the local school and town dignitaries, students, and a Nobel prize winner, Professor D. Herschbach of Harvard University as the principal speaker. The program also included short comments by me and by my nephew, "Gil" Lewis, who is professor of mathematics at Michigan Tech. On a state wide level Oct. 23, 1993 was proclaimed by Governor Weld as Gilbert Newton Lewis Day throughout Massachusetts[237]. Not content to stop there, Paretchan convinced Senator Edward Kennedy of Lewis' distinction enough so that the senator gave a speech to the senate on the subject[238]. Efforts for still wider recognition continue. Mr. Paretchan has corresponded with the Nobel Prize committee to try to get them to give a posthumous prize, which they explained was without precedent. Although Mr. Paretchan pointed out that this had been done in one case, which they conceded. However, at the time the committee met to decide on the awards the nominee was still alive, but died before the formal award ceremony.

He has lobbied, by correspondence, the president's office with the aim of having Lewis awarded a Presidential Medal of Freedom and/or the Presidential Citizens Medal. Paretchan has also worked on Congress for the award of the Congressional Gold Medal. He has also recommended a G. N. Lewis stamp, so far unsuccessfully, but is continuing this effort. He nominated Lewis for the Hall of Fame for Great Americans, only to find out that this distinction has not been in business for many years. He attempted to get two television programs to run a program on Lewis without success. The amount of letter writing that has gone into these efforts is staggering.

Harold Paretchan's efforts have not gone unnoticed. The local Weymouth press has had several articles describing his various local and national efforts. The governor's proclamation of Oct 23, 1993 as Gilbert Newton Lewis Day received more than local coverage. An article in Chemical and Engineering News[239] has been written, and University of California articles, especially those from the College of Chemistry, have appeared. He has traveled to California and visited the University and the Chemistry department briefly. He has received the unprecedented distinction of being named honorary member of the "Alumni of the Gilbert Newton Lewis Era," at the Berkeley department.

Mr. Paretchan has written to virtually all living chemistry Nobel prize winners in chemistry to ask their opinions of Lewis. The level of response has been impressive, and excerpts from some of these letters follow. I include a letter from Daniel Koshland in this group because (although not a Nobel winner) he is very distinguished, and unlike most of the others in this collection, he was an undergraduate at Berkeley in Lewis' time. Also included is a letter to Lewis from Ernest Rutherford, who died in 1937, well before Paretchan's search. In addition to those quoted here, a number recognized Lewis as a distinguished name in chemistry, but had no personal knowledge of him or his work. The only negative letter is the one from D. J. Cram, who did not like Lewis' neglect of organic chemistry. There is no significance to the order of these quotations. In all the letters, many but by no means all references to Lewis's contributions to the electron pair bond, Lewis acids, thermodynamics, deuterium, and the triplet state have been extensively edited, avoiding repetitive opinions.

"Though I did not know G. N. Lewis, it has become clear to me that his creative, intuitive spirit was one of the major determinants of the preeminence of USA chemistry..... Lewis combined creatively teaching, masterful exposition and truly original research".

> Roald Hoffmann
> Nobel Prize in Chemistry
> 1981

"Gilbert Newton Lewis was undoubtedly one of the most outstanding historical figures in chemistry.....[He] truly ranks among the immortals of science".   Dudley Herschbach
> Nobel Prize in Chemistry
> 1986

Herbert Brown describes how his own research nearly stopped after he was appointed as assistant professor at Wayne University, which offered practically nothing in the way of research support at that time. However, on learning about Lewis' research in Manila on silver oxide done with the minimum of equipment, Brown was able to make some tertiary alkyl chlorides and measure their hydrolysis rates, also with almost no equipment to start to his career in steric effects, culminating in his Prize.

> Herbert C. Brown
> Nobel Prize in Chemistry
> 1979

I consider him one of the greatest chemists this country has ever produced, and in his own way as great as Linus Pauling, who by any measure is a giant.

> Henry Taube
> Nobel Prize in Chemistry
> 1983

I never met G. N. Lewis, and knew him only by reputation, which was "larger than life".... G. N. Lewis, by reputation, dominated the Berkeley Chemistry Department for years, and built up the physical chemistry part of it..... He did not regard organic chemistry as a science, and hired but one organic chemist for years. As a result, it was only long after his death that Organic Chemistry at Berkeley flourished. He inhibited its growth there for probably 20 years....

> Donald J. Cram
> Nobel Prize in Chemistry
> 1987

G. N. Lewis was certainly one of the century's greatest chemists. I have a framed portrait of him in my office, and carry it to class when I lecture about his work in general chemistry.

> Thomas R. Cech
> Nobel Prize in Chemistry
> 1989

Dr. Lewis was one of the great giants of chemistry. His ideas of valence and electron distribution in molecules provided a simple cohesive theory that changed the understanding of chemistry..... He was a great innovator and a fine scholar...

> Daniel E. Koshland Jr.
> Former Editor, "Science"
> National Medal of Science
> 1991

Lewis is truly a household name among chemists......

The Chemistry Department at the University of California at Berkeley was built into one of the very finest in the world through the sustained effort and wisdom of G. N. Lewis. As an alumnus of the graduate program, I am very proud of my alma mater.

The preface to *Thermodynamics* , shows the imaginative and poetic element in the personality of G. N. Lewis. That magnificent piece of prose is a marvelous description of the human nature of the scientific enterprise.

> Robert F. Curl
> Nobel Prize in Chemistry
> 1996

I consider G. N. Lewis to have been one of the greatest chemists of the world, of the previous generation.

> Linus Pauling

Nobel Prize in Chemistry
1954

I have often been asked to identify the ablest and greatest scientist that I have known personally during my career as a scientist (now extending over 60 years). I unhesitatingly designate Lewis as one of the two best that I have known (the other being the extraordinary physicist Enrico Fermi), (and in Chemical and Engineering News, **1993**, Nov. 1 p27) "I was awestruck as I worked with him. Wherever he turned, his great intellect penetrated the field and solved the problem".

Glenn T. Seaborg
Nobel Prize in Chemistry
1951

I never had any direct contact with [G. N. Lewis] unfortunately, but he has touched my life in several ways. Certainly his numerous important contributions to chemistry, such as the concept of the electron pair bond, the generalized concept of an acid and a base, his very excellent work in spectroscopy and his profound contributions to thermodynamics are some examples of how G. N. Lewis influenced the scientific thoughts of most chemists.

Jerome Karle
Nobel prize in Chemistry
1985

A letter from Yuan Tseh Lee describes how he spent a summer in Taiwan studying thermodynamics from Lewis and Randall and developing an admiration for Lewis. When he came to Berkeley for graduate school in 1962 Lewis was no longer there but his legacy and influence were still very much alive. Lee was impressed by the persistence of the idea that doing research at the earliest possible time was one of these legacies, and he felt that he had known Lewis well both from the early study experience and the still persistent influence.

Yuan Tseh Lee
Nobel Prize in Chemistry
1986

Letters from Melvin Calvin (Nobel prize in Chemistry, 1961) and from Michael Kasha show admiration and respect; this is shown elsewhere.

My feeling was then [1933-1937] and now that Prof. Lewis was at the core of our current understanding and use of thermodynamic principles.

Christian B. Anfinsen
Nobel Prize in Chemistry, 1972

Lewis was a pioneering U. S. scientist whose contributions had a profound influence on chemistry education and research in this country and a strong influence on me personally. The book and work of Lewis and Randall in chemical thermodynamics, Lewis' concept of the electron pair bond, his equally pioneering work on triplet states of organic molecules, his generalization of the concepts of acids and bases, all are still with us today and play an important role in our thinking.

Rudolph A. Marcus
Nobel Prize in Chemistry
1992

I was surprised to learn that he never was awarded a Nobel prize.....But I consider it as being more important that the phrases Lewis acid and Lewis base will continue to be used even in times when the names of Nobel Prize winners will be forgotten.

Hartmut Michel
Nobel Prize in Chemistry
1988

All I can say is that he was indeed a great pioneering chemist whose ideas changed the face of chemistry. Most people in chemistry will know his name best for Lewis acids and bases, of course.

Geoffrey Wilkinson
Nobel Prize in Chemistry
1973

I still have on my shelves a copy of Lewis and Randall, Thermodynamics,..... my first introduction to that subject. And of course much of one's studies revolved around the nature of the chemical bond, and in the generation before Pauling there is no doubt that G. N. Lewis was the commanding figure. He was certainly a very great chemist

> Sir John Kendrew
> Nobel Prize in Chemistry
> 1962

Since I am an Organic Chemist, I would like to testify that Organic Chemists use his name almost every day of their working lives when they refer to "Lewis acids" as catalysts.

> D. H. R. Barton
> Nobel Prize in Chemistry
> 1969

G. N. Lewis was a true giant of chemistry and I am still puzzled why he was not given the Nobel Prize, which he richly deserved. My own research on very acidic systems (superacids) and their chemistry was directly inspired by Lewis' pioneering work and ideas.

> George A. Olah
> Nobel prize in Chemistry
> 1994

We are all no doubt in his debt in regard to his deep insight into nature.

> Kenichi Fukui
> Nobel Prize in Chemistry
> 1981

His concepts of acids and bases contributed greatly to my thinking about organic reaction mechanisms during the phase of my career when I was doing synthetic organic chemistry. I can only concur with those, such as Linus Pauling, who knew Lewis personally and who knew his research intimately, in saying that he was a towering figure in chemistry in the middle of the twentieth century and that he had a major impact at a time when synthetic organic chemistry was undergoing one of its most productive periods.

Michael Smith
Nobel Prize in Chemistry
1993

A letter from Lipscomb summarizes in some detail the original Lewis picture of bonding; it also describes the process by which this became rationalized with the new quantum mechanics. Then the utility of activity and fugacity are described. "In his last several years he carried out studies of fluorescence and phosphorescence. I presented a colloquium on one of these studies by Lewis and Kasha in 1945 at Cal Tech where I was completing a PhD Thesis.

This experience, my solution of most of the problem sets in Thermodynamics by Lewis and Randall, and my exposure to the further developments of the chemical bond by Pauling, all led me to feel that I knew G. N. Lewis well, although I never had occasion to meet him."

William N. Lipscomb
Nobel Prize in Chemistry
1976

I have long been an admirer of G. N. Lewis. He was a major power in American chemistry during the first half of this century, and one of the world's most outstanding physical chemists... He was an unique scientist with a powerful personality to go along with his enormous intellect.

E. J. Corey
Nobel Prize in Chemistry
1990

....I remember having difficulties understanding some basic concepts in thermodynamics, until I discovered his text, written with M. Randall, which had a very large influence in my formation as a physical chemist.

I should also note that Dr. Lewis had a great influence on his colleagues and students; my PhD. mentor at Berkeley, Professor George Pimentel, used to speak very fondly of him. There is little doubt that Dr. Gilbert Newton Lewis was one of the great chemists of this century,

Mario J. Molina
Nobel Prize in Chemistry, 1995

Another letter from a Nobel prize winner came to Lewis too ealy for Paretchan's collection, but this seems to be the place to put it. It was dated May 30, 1933.

"I have been enormously interested in your work of concentration of the new isotope with almost unbelievable success. I congratulate you and your staff on this splendid performance. I can appreciate the extraordinary value of this new element in opening up a new type of chemistry. If I were a younger man I think I would leave everything else to examine the effects produced by the substitution of H^2 for H^1 in all reactions. . .

With best wishes to you all and good success to your labours; and my most grateful thanks for your splendid gift.
Yours very sincerely

Rutherford"
Nobel Prize in Chemistry
1908

This letter is quoted from Lachman [204], the splendid gift refers to a sample of heavy water, one of those which Lewis sent out to a number of laboratories throughout the world after the isolation became practical on a slightly larger scale.

References

Lewis papers are Nos.1-168, other authors are Nos. 201 on. Before 1910, Lewis often published the same paper in more than one journal. In most cases this was in German, and this was apparently a custom at that time.

1. Some electrochemical and thermochemical relations of zinc and cadmium amalgams (with T. W. Richards). *Proc. Amer. Acad.* 1898, *34*, 87. *Z. phys. Chem.* 1899, *28*, 1.

2. The development and application of a general equation for free energy and physico-chemical equilibrium. *Proc. Amer Acad.* 1899, *35*, 3. *Z. phys. Chem.* 1900, *32*, 364.

3. A new conception of thermal pressure and a theory of solutions. *Proc. Amer Acad.* 1900, *36*, 145. *Z. phys. Chem.* 1900, *35*, 343.

4. The law of physico-chemical change. *Proc. Amer. Acad.* 1901, *37*, 49. *Z. phys. Chem.* 1901, *38*, 205.

5. The autocatalytic decomposition of silver oxide. *Proc. Amer. Acad.* 1905, *40*, 719. *Bull. Gov. Lab. P. I.* 1905, 30.

6. Hydration in solution. *Z. physik. Chem.* 1905, *52*, 224. *Bull. Gov. Lab. Manila, P.I.* 1905, 30.

7. Concerning silver oxide and silver suboxide. *J. Am. Chem. Soc.* 1906, *28*, 139. *Phillipine J. Sci.* 1906, *1*, 439. *Z. phys. Chem.* 1906, *55*, 449.

8. The potential of the oxygen electrode. *J. Am. Chem. Soc.* 1906, *28*, 465. *Z. phys. Chem.* 1906, *55*, 465.

9. Galvanic polarization on a mercury cathode (with R. F. Jackson). *Proc. Amer. Acad.* 1906, *41*, 399. *Z. phys. Chem.* 1906, *56*, 193.

10. The electrical conductivity of solutions in liquid iodine (with P. Wheeler). *Proc. Amer. Acad.* 1906, *41*, 419. *Z. phys. Chem.* 1906, *56*, 179.

11. Über Komplexbildung, Hydratation und Farbe. *Z. physik. Chem.* 1906, *56*, 223.

12. An elementary proof of the relation between the vapor pressure and the composition of a binary mixture. *J. Amer. Chem. Soc.* 1906, *28*, 569.

13. On the applicability of Raoult's law to molecular weight determinations in mixed solvents and in simple solvents whose vapor dissociates. *J. Am. Chem. Soc.* 1906, *28*, 766.

14. A review of recent progress in physical chemistry. *J. Am. Chem. Soc.* 1906, *28*, 893.

15. Equilibrium in the Deacon process. *J. Am. Chem. Soc.* 1906, *28*, 1380.

16. The specific heat of solids at constant volume, and the law of Dulong and Petit. *J. Am. Chem. Soc.* 1907, *29*, 1163. *Z. anorg. Chem.* 1907, *55*, 200.

17. Outlines of a new system of thermodynamic chemistry. *Proc. Amer. Acad.* **1907**, *43*, 259. *Z. phys. Chem.* **1907**, *61*, 129.

18. The osmotic pressure of concentrated solutions, and the laws of perfect solution. *J. Am. Chem. Soc.* **1908**, *30*, 668. *Chem. News*, **1908**, *99*, 40.

19. The determination of ionic hydration from electromotive force. *J. Am. Chem. Soc.* **1908**, *30*, 1355. *Z. Elektrochem,* **1908**, *14*, 509.

20. A revision of the fundamental laws of matter and energy. *Phil. Mag.* **1908**, *16*, 705. *Technol. Quart.* **1908**, *21*, 212. *Ann. Naturphil.* **1908**, *7*, 429.

21. The ionic theory. *Sch.Sci. Math* . **1908**, *8*, 484.

22. The potential of the ferro-ferricyanide electrode (with L. W. Sargent). *J. Am. Chem. Soc.* **1909**, *31*, 355.

23. Potentials between liquids (with L. W. Sargent) *J. Am. Chem. Soc.* **1909**, *31*, 363.

24. The principle of relativity and non-Newtonian mechanics (with R. C. Tolman) *Proc. Amer. Acad.* **1909**, *44*, 711. *Phil. Mag.* **1909**, *18*, 510.

25. The fundamental laws of matter and energy. *Science,* **1909**, *30*, 84.

26. The use and abuse of ionic theory. *Science,* **1909**, *30*, 1. *Z. Phys, Chem,.* **1909**, 212

27. The potential of the thallium electrode (with C. L. von Ende). *J. Am. Chem. Soc.* **1910**, *32*, 732.

28. The theory of the determination of transference numbers by the method of moving boundaries. *J. Am. Chem. Soc.* **1910** *32*, 862.

29. On four-dimensional vector analysis and its application in electrical theory. *Proc. Amer. Acad.* **1910**, *46*, 165. *Jb. Radioakt.* **1910**, *7*, 329.

30. The potential of the sodium electrode (with C. A. Kraus). *J. Am. Chem. Soc.* **1910**, *32*, 1459.

31. The equilibrium between nitric acid, nitrous acid and nitric oxide (with A. Edgar). *J. Am. Chem. Soc.* **1911**, *33*, 292.

32. The potential of the chlorine electrode (with F. R. Rupert). *J. Am. Chem. Soc.* **1911**, *33*, 299.

33. The heat content of the various forms of sulfur (with M. Randall). *J. Am. Chem. Soc.* **1911**, *33*, 476.

34. The potential of the potassium electrode (with F. G. Keyes). *J. Am. Chem. Soc.* **1912**, *34*, 119.

35. The equilibrium between ammonium carbonate and ammonium carbamate in aqueous solution at 25∞ (with G. H. Burrows). *J. Am. Chem. Soc.* **1912**, *34*, 993.

36. A summary of the specific heats of gases (with M. Randall). *J. Am. Chem. Soc.* **1912**, *34*, 1515.

37. The free energy of organic compounds. I. The reversible synthesis of urea and of ammonium cyanate (with G. H. Burrows). *J. Am. Chem. Soc.* **1912,** *34,* 1515.

38. The space-time manifold of relativity; the non-Euclidean geometry of mechanics and electromagnetics (with E. B. Wilson). *Proc. Amer. Acad.* **1912,** *48,* 389.

39. The activity of ions and the degree of dissociation of strong electrolytes. *J. Am. Chem. Soc.* **1912,** *34,* 1631.

40. The free energy of chemical substances. *J. Am. Chem. Soc.* **1913,** *35,* 1.

41. The potential of the lithium electrode (with F. G. Keyes). *J. Am Chem. Soc.* **1913,** *35,* 340.

42. Valence and tautomerism. *J. Am. Chem. Soc.* **1913,** *35,* 1448.

43. Notes on quantum theory: A theory of ultimate rational units; numerical relations between elementary charge, Wirkungsquantum, constant of Stefan's law (with E. Q. Adams). *Phys. Rev.* **1914,** *3,* 92.

44. The potential of the copper electrode and the activity of bi-valent ions (with W. N. Lacey). *J. Am. Chem. Soc.* **1914,** *36,* 804.

45. Notes on quantum theory: The distribution of thermal energy (with E. Q. Adams). *Phys. Rev.* **1914,** *4,* 331.

46. The free energy of oxygen, hydrogen and the oxides of hydrogen (with M. Randall). *J. Am. Chem. Soc.* **1914,** *36,* 1969.

47. The free energy of iodine compounds (with M. Randall). *J. Am. Chem. Soc.* **1914,** *36,* 2259.

48. The free energy of various forms of elemental sulfur (with M. Randall). *J. Am. Chem. Soc.* **1914,** *36,* 2468.

49. The free energy of some carbon compounds (with M. Randall). *J. Am. Chem. Soc.* **1915,** *37,* 458.

50. The Maxwell distribution law in Newtonian and non-Newtonian mechanics (with E. Q. Adams). *Phys. Rev.* **1915,** *5,* 510.

51. The equilibrium between carbon oxysulfide, carbon monoxide and sulfur (with W. N. Lacey). *J. Am. Chem. Soc.* **1915,** *37,* 1976.

52. The potential of the rubidium electrode (with W. L. Argo). *J. Am. Chem. Soc.* **1915,** *37,* 1983.

53. The free energy of nitrogen compounds (with E. Q. Adams). *J. Am. Chem. Soc.* **1915,** *37,* 2308.

54 Electrical transference in amalgams (with E. Q. Adams and E. H. Lanman) *J. Am. Chem. Soc.* **1915,** *37,* 2656.

55. The atom and the molecule. *J. Am. Chem. Soc.* **1916,** *38,* 762.

56. Steric hindrance and the existence of odd molecules. *Proc. Nat. Acad. Sci.* **1916,** *2,* 586.

57. The free energy of bromine compounds (with M. Randall). *J. Am. Chem. Soc.* **1916,** *38,* 2348.

58. Electrical conductance in dilute amalgams (with T. B. Hine). *Proc. Nat. Acad. Sci.* **1916,** *2,* 634.

59. The potential of the lead electrode (with T. B. Brighton). *J. Am. Chem. Soc.* **1917,** *39,* 1906.

60. The static atom. *Science.* **1917,** *46,* 297.

61. A study of hydrogen and calomel electrodes (with T. B. Brighton and R. L. Sebastian). *J. Am. Chem. Soc.* **1917,** *39,* 2245.

62. The potential of the bromine electrode; the free energy of dilution of hydrogen bromide; the distribution of bromide between several phases (with H. Storch). *J. Am. Chem. Soc.* **1917,** *39,* 2544.

63. The entropy of the elements and the third law of thermodynamics (with G. E. Gibson). *J. Am. Chem. Soc.* **1917,** *39,* 2554.

64. A preliminary study of reversible reactions of sulfur compounds (with M. Randall and E. R. von Bichowsky). *J. Am. Chem. Soc.* **1918,** *40,* 356.

65. Equilibrium in the reaction between water and sulfur at the boiling point of sulfur (with M. Randall). *J. Am. Chem. Soc.* **1918,** *40,* 362.

66. The heat capacity of electropositive metals and the thermal energy of free electrons (with E. D. Eastman and W. H. Rodebush). *Proc. Nat. Acad. Sci.* **1918,** *4,* 25.

67. Equilibria involving cyanogen iodide; the free energy of formation of cyanogen (with D. B. Keyes). *J. Am. Chem. Soc.* **1918,** *40,* 472.

68. The oxidizing power of cyanates and the free energy of formation of cyanides (with T. B. Brighton). *J. Am. Chem. Soc.* **1918,** *40,* 482.

69. The degree of ionization of very dilute electrolytes (with G. A. Linhart). *J. Am. Chem. Soc.* **1919,** *41,* 1951.

70. The third law of thermodynamics and the entropy of solutions and of liquids (with G. E. Gibson). *J. Am. Chem. Soc.* **1920,** *42,* 1529.

71. The thermodynamic treatment of concentrated solutions and applications to thallium amalgams (with M. Randall). *J. Am. Chem. Soc.* **1921,** *43,* 233.

72. Color and chemical constitution. *Chem. Met. Eng.* **1921** *24* , 871.

73. The activity coefficients of strong electrolytes (with M. Randall) *J. Am. Chem. Soc.* **1921,** *43,* 1112.

74. A revision of the entropies of the elements (with G. E. Gibson and W. M. Latimer) *J. Am.. Chem. Soc.* **1922,** *44,* 1008.

75. The chemistry of the stars and the evolution of radioactive substances, *Publ. Astron. Soc. Pacific,* **1922,** *34,* 309.

76. Physical constants and the ultimate rational units, *Phil. Mag.* **1923,** *45,* 266. *Contrib. Jefferson Physical Lab.* **1922,** *15,* no. 21.

77. Thermodynamics and the free energy of chemical substances (with M. Randall) McGraw-Hill Book Company, New York, 1923.

78. Valence and the structure of atoms and molecules. The Chemical Catalog Company, New York, 1923.

79. Valence and the electron. *Trans. Faraday Soc.* **1923,** *19,* 452.

80. Extremely dry liquids. *J. Am. Chem. Soc.* **1923,** *45,* 2836.

81. The magnetochemical theory. *Chem. Rev.* **1924,** *1,* 233.

82. The magnetism of oxygen and the molecule O_4. *J. Am. Chem. Soc.* **1924,** *46,* 2027.

83. Europas skulder och mynfoten. *Finsk Tidskrift,* **1924,** December.

84. A new principle of equilibrium. *Proc. Nat. Acad. Sci.* **1925,** *11,* 179.

85. A plan for stabilizing prices. *The Economic Journal,* **1925,** *35,* 170.

86. Ultimate rational units and dimensional theory, *Phil. Mag.,* **1925,** *49,* 739.

87. The theory of reaction rate (with D. F. Smith). *J. Am. Chem. Soc.* **1925,** *47,* 1508.

88. The distribution of energy in thermal radiation and the law of entire equilibrium. *Proc. Nat. Acad. Sci.* **1925,** *11,* 422.

89. The paramagnetism of "odd molecules". (with N. W. Taylor). *Proc. Nat. Acad. Sci.* **1925,** *11,* 456.

90. The nature of light. *Proc. Nat. Acad. Sci.* **1926,** *12,* 22.

91. Light waves and light corpuscles. *Nature,* **1926,** *117,* 236.

92. The path of light quanta in an interference field. *Proc. Nat Acad. Sci.* **1926,** *12,* 439.

93 The anatomy of science. Yale University Press, New Haven, 1926.

94. The conservation of photons. *Nature,* **1926,** *118,* 874.

95 The entropy of radiation. *Proc. Nat. Acad. Sci.* **1927,** *13,* 307.

96. A new equation for the distribution of radiant energy. *Proc. Nat. Acad. Sci.* **1927,** *13,* 471.

97. A disproof of the radiation theory of chemical activation. *Proc. Nat. Acad. Sci.* **1927,** *13,* 623.

98. Entropy at infinite pressure and the equation of state of solids. *Z. physik. Chem. (Cohen Festband),* **1927,** *130,* 532.

99. Natural radioactivity and the origin of species (with A. R. Olson), *Nature,* **1928,** *121,* 673.

100. Thermodynamics based on statistics. I. (with J. E. Mayer). *Proc. Nat. Acad. Sci.* **1928,** *14,* 569.

101. Thermodynamics based on statistics. II. (with J. E. Mayer). *Proc. Nat. Acad. Sci.* **1928,** *14,* 575.

102. The quantum laws and the uncertainty principle of Heisenberg (with J. E. Mayer). *Proc. Nat. Acad. Sci.* **1929,** *15,* 2.

103. The thermodynamics of gases which show degeneracy (Entartung) (with J. E. Mayer). *Proc. Nat. Acad . Sci.* **1929,** *15,* 208.

104. The symmetry of time in physics. *Science,* **1930,** *71,* 569.

105. Quantum kinetics and the Planck equation. *Phys. Rev.* **1930,** *35,* 1533.

106. The principle of identity and the exclusion of quantum states. *Phys. Rev.* **1930,** *36,* 1144.

107. Generalized thermodynamics including the theory of fluctuations.. *J. Am Chem. Soc.* **1931,** *53,* 2578.

108. A more fundamental thermodynamics. *Phys. Rev.* **1931,** *38,* 376.

109. The chemical bond. *J. Chem. Phys.* 1933, *1,* 17.

110. The isotope of hydrogen. *J. Am. Chem. Soc.* 1933, *55,* 1297.

111. Concentration of the H^2 isotope (with R. T. Macdonald). *J. Chem. Phys.* **1933,** *1,* 341.

112. Separation of the isotopic forms of water by fractional distillation (with R. E. Cornish). *J. Am. Chem. Soc.* **1933,** *55,* 2216.

113. Spin of hydrogen isotope (with M. E. Ashley). *Phys. Rev.* **1933,** *49,* 837.

114. A spectroscopic search for H^3 in concentrated H^2 (with E. H. Spedding). *Phys. Rev.* **1933,** *43,* 964.

115. The emission of alpha-particles from various targets bombarded by deutons of high speed (with M. S. Livingston and E. O. Lawrence) *Phys. Rev.* **1933**, *44*, 55.

116 The emission of protons from various targets bombarded by deutons of high speed (with E. O. Lawrence and M. S. Livingston). *Phys. Rev.* **1933**, *44*, 56.

117. Some properties of H^2H^2O (with R. T. Macdonald). *J. Am. Chem. Soc.* **1933**, *55*, 3057.

118. A simple type of isotopic reaction. *J. Am. Chem. Soc.* **1933**, *55*, 3057.

119. The biochemistry of water containing hydrogen isotope. *J. Am. Chem. Soc.* **1933**, *55*, 3503.

120. The mobility of ions in H^2H^2O (with T. C. Doody). *J. Am. Chem. Soc.* **1933**, *55*, 3504.

121. The viscosity of H^2H^2O (with R. T. Macdonald). *J. Am. Chem. Soc.* **1933**, *55*, 4730.

122. The dielectric constant of H^2H^2O (with A. R. Olson and W. Maroney). *J. Am. Chem. Soc.* **1933**, *55*, 4731.

123. The refractive index of H_2O^{18} and the complete isotopic analysis of water (with D. B. Luten). *J. Am. Chem. Soc.* **1933**, *55*, 5061.

124, The biology of heavy water. *Science,* **1934**, *79*, 151.

125. The disintegration of deutons by high speed protons and the instability of the deuton (with M. S. Livingston, M. C. Henderson and E. O. Lawrence). *Phys. Rev.* **1934**, *45*, 493.

126. Some properties of pure deutacetic acid (with P. W. Schutz). *J. Am. Chem. Soc.* **1934**, *56*, 493.

127. The vapor pressure of liquid and solid deutochloric acid (with R. T. Macdonald and P. W. Schutz). *J. Am. Chem. Soc.* **1934**, *56*, 494.

128. The vapor pressure of mixtures of light and heavy hydrogen (with W. T. Hanson). *J. Am. Chem. Soc.* **1934**, *56*, 1000.

129. The vapor pressure of solid and liquid heavy hydrogen (with W. T. Hanson). *J. Am. Chem. Soc.* **1934**, *56*, 1001.

130. The vapor pressure of liquid and solid deutocyanic acid (with P. W. Schutz). *J. Am. Chem. Soc.* **1934**, *56*, 1002.

131. The ionization constant of deutacetic acid (with P. W. Schutz). *J. Am. Chem. Soc.* **1934**, *56*, 1002.

132. On the hypothesis of the instability of the deuton (with M. S. Livingston, M. C. Henderson and E. O. Lawrence). *Phys Rev.* **1934**, *45*, 497.

133. Different kinds of water. *IX Congreso Internacional de Quimica,* Madrid, April, 1934.

134. The vapor pressure of solid and liquid deuterium and the heats of sublimation, of fusion and of vaporization (with W. T. Hanson). *J. Am. Chem. Soc*. **1934**, *56*, 1687.

135. The ionization of some weak electrolytes in heavy water (with P. W. Schutz). *J. Am. Chem. Soc.* **1934**, *56*, 1913.

136. The genesis of the elements *Phys. Rev.* **1934**, *46*, 897.

137. A theory of orbital neutrons. *Phys. Rev.* **1936**, *50*, 857.

138. The separation of lithium isotopes (with R. T. Macdonald). *J. Am. Chem. Soc.* **1936**, *58*, 2519.

139. Refraction of neutrons (with P. W. Schutz). *Phys. Rev.* **1937**, *51*, 369.

140. Neutron optics. *Phys. Rev.* **1937**, *51*, 371.

141. Neutron refraction (with P. W. Schutz). *Phys. Rev.* **1937**, *51*, 1105.

142. Review of "A Commentary on the Scientific Writings of J. Willard Gibbs," edited by F. G. Donnan and Arthur Haas. *J. Am. Chem. Soc.* **1937**, *59*, 2749.

143. Acids and bases, *J. Franklin Inst.* **1938**, *226*, 293.

144. Primary and secondary acids and bases (with G. T. Seaborg). *J. Am. Chem. Soc.* **1939**, *61*, 1886.

145. Trinitrotriphenylmethide ion as a secondary and primary base (with G. T. Seaborg). *J. Am. Chem. Soc.* **1939**, *61*, 1894.

146. The color of organic substances (with M. Calvin). *Chem. Rev.* **1939**, *25*, 273.

147. The acidity of aromatic nitro compounds toward amines. The effect of double chelation (with G. T. Seaborg). *J. Am. Chem. Soc.* **1940**, *62*, 2122.

148. The absorption and re-emission of light by *cis* and *trans*-stilbenes and the efficiency of their photochemical isomerization (with T. T. Magel and D. Lipkin). *J. Am. Chem. Soc.* **1940**, *62*, 2973.

149. The dissociation of tetraphenylhydrazine and its derivatives (with D. Lipkin). *J. Am. Chem. Soc.* **1941**, *63*, 3232.

150. Reversible photochemical processes in rigid media. A study of the phosphorescent state (with D. Lipkin and T. T. Magel). *J. Am. Chem. Soc.* **1941**, *63*, 3005.

151. Isomers of crystal violet ion. Their absorption and re-emission of light (with T. T. Magel and D. Lipkin). *J. Am. Chem. Soc.* **1942**, *64*, 1774.

152. Reversible photochemical processes in rigid media: The dissociation of organic molecules into radicals and ions (with D. Lipkin). *J. Am. Chem. Soc.* **1942**, *64*, 2801.

153. The initial step in the action of acids on tetraarylhdrazines (with J. Bigeleisen). *J. Am. Chem. Soc.* **1942**, *64*, 2808.

154. The orientation of molecules produced photochemically in rigid solvents (with J. Bigeleisen). *J. Am. Chem. Soc.* **1943**, *65*, 520.

155. Methylene blue and other indicators in general acids. The acidity function (with J.

Bigeleisen). *J. Am. Chem. Soc.* **1943**, *65*, 1044.

156. Dimeric and other forms of methylene blue: Absorption and fluorescence of the pure monomer (with O. Goldschmid, T. T. Magel and J. Bigeleisen). *J. Am. Chem. Soc.* **1943**, *65*, 1150.

157. The second order *x* bands in absorption spectra (with J. Bigeleisen). *J. Am. Chem. Soc.* **1943**, *65*, 2107.

158. The *y* bands in absorption spectra (with J. Bigeleisen). *J. Am. Chem. Soc.* **1943**, *65*, 2102.

159. Photochemical reactions of leuco dyes in rigid solvents. Quantum efficiency of photo-oxidation (with J. Bigeleisen). *J. Am. Chem. Soc.* **1943**, *65*, 2419.

160. Further photo-oxidation in rigid media (with J. Bigeleisen). *J. Am. Chem. Soc.* **1943**, *65*, 2424.

161. The light absorption and fluorescence of triarylmethyl free radicals (with D. Lipkin and T. T. Magel). *J. Am. Chem. Soc.* **1944**, *66*, 1579.

162. Phosphorescence and the triplet state (with M. Kasha). *J. Am. Chem. Soc.* **1944**, *66*, 2100.

163. Rules for the absorption spectra of dyes. *J. Am. Chem. Soc.* **1945**, *67*, 770.

164. Phosphorescence in fluid media and the reverse process of singlet-triplet absorption (with M. Kasha). *J. Am. Chem. Soc.* **1945**, *67*, 994.

165. Paramagnetism of the phosphorescent state (with M. Calvin). *J. Am. Chem. Soc.* **1945**, *67*, 1232.

166. Thermodynamics of an ice age: The cause and sequence of glaciation. *Science.* **1946**, *104*, 43.

167. The beginning of civilization in America. *American Anthropologist,* **1947**, *49*, 1.

168. Paramagnetism of the triplet state (With M. Calvin and M. Kasha). *J. Chem. Phys.* **1949**, *17*, 804.

Reference numbers from 200 on are to authors other than G. N. Lewis.

201. W. L. Jolly, "From Retorts to Lasers; The Story of Chemistry at Berkeley". Distributed by the College of Chemistry, University of California, Berkeley, CA 94720.

202. "In Honor of Gilbert Newton Lewis on his Seventieth Birthday". Printed by the University of California Press, Berkeley, 1945. It contains an almost complete Lewis publication list. This anonymous publication also contains a list of all PhDs granted by the department fom 1914 to 1945.

203. J. H. Hildebrand, *Biographical Memoirs of the National Academy of Sciences,* **1958**,*31*, 210.

112

204. A. Lachman, "Borderland of the Unknown; the Life story of Gilbert Newton Lewis." Pageant Press, 1955.

205. R. N. Lewis, "A Pioneer Spirit from a Pioneer Family", *J. Chem. Ed.* **1984**, *61*, 3.

206. From the City of Houston Clayton Library for Genealogical research. I am indebted to the library staff for help in finding this information.

207. G. Fleck, Chapter on S. Arrhenius in *Nobel Laureates in Chemistry*, L. K. James Ed., American Chemical Society, 1993.

208. G. Fleck, Chapter on T. W. Richards in *Nobel Laureates in Chemistry*, L. K. James, Ed., American Chemical Society, 1993

209. 1880 Massachusetts census, courtesy of Harold Paretchan.

210. Harvard College, Class of 1896 - Report VI, 1921.

211. J. W. Servos, "G. N. Lewis: The Disciplinary Setting", *J. Chem. Ed.* **1984**, *61*, 5.

212. Harvard College, Class of 1896 Fiftieth Anniversary Report , 1946.

213. From the Lewis archives in the U. of California library, retrieved by my nephew, G. N. Lewis.

214. Much more of the history of San Francisco than is relevant here is in the book "Golden Gate" by Felix Reisenberg, Jr. Tudor Publishing Co. New York, 1940.

215. M. Calvin and G. T Seaborg, "The College of Chemistry in the G. N. Lewis Era", *J. Chem. Ed.*, **1984**, *61*, 11.

216. ACS Directory of Graduate Research, American Chemical Society, 1989. Other issues of this directory will show a similar count.

217. K. S. Pitzer and L. Brewer, "Thermodynamics", a second edition of G. N. Lewis and M. Randall, "Thermodynamics and the Free Energies of Chemical Substances" McGraw-Hill, New York 1961.

218. K. S. Pitzer, "Gilbert N. Lewis and the Thermodynamics of Strong Electrolytes", *J. Chem. Ed.*, **1984**, *61*, 104.

219. W. C. Bray and G. E. K. Branch "Valence and Tautomerism" *J. Am. Chem. Soc.* **1913**, *35* , 1444.

220. W. B. Jensen, "Abegg, Lewis, Langmuir, and the Octet Rule", *J. Chem. Ed.* **1984**, *61*, 191.

221. R. E. Kohler, "The Origins of G. N. Lewis's Theory of the Shared Pair Bond", *Historical Studies in the Physical Sciences*, **1971**, *3*, 343. Quoted from a letter from Ostwald to Richards 3/30/1901 in the T. W. Richards archives, Harvard University.

222. A. N. Stranges, "Reflections on the electron theory of the chemical bond; 1900-192," *J. Chem. Ed.*, **1984**, *61*, 185.

223. L. Pauling, "G. N. Lewis and the Chemical Bond", *J. Chem. Ed.* **1984**, *61*, 201.

224. M. Calvin, " Gilbert Newton Lewis. His Influence on Physical-Organic Chemists at

Berkeley", *J. Chem. Ed.* **1984,** *61,* 14.

225. J. Bigeleisen, "Gilbert N. Lewis and the Beginnings of Isotope Chemistry", *J. Chem. Ed.,* **1984,** *61,* 108.

226. W. F. Libby, "Tritium in Nature," *J. Wash. Acad. Sci.* **1955,** *45,* 91.

227. G. T. Seaborg, "The Research Style of Gilbert N. Lewis", *J. Chem. Ed.* **1984,** *61,* 93.

228. G. T. Seaborg, "Gilbert Newton Lewis--Some Personal Recollections of a Chemical Giant" *The Chemical Intelligencer* , **1995,** 27.

229. L. Brewer, "The Generalized Lewis Acid-Base Theory", *J. Chem. Ed.* **1984,** *61,* 101.

230. M. Kasha, "The Triplet State: An Example Of G. N. Lewis' Research Style", *J. Chem. Ed.* **1984,** *61,* 204.

231. M. Calvin, "Gilbert Newton Lewis", Welch Foundation Conference on Chemical Research XX. American Chemistry-Bicentennial 1976, Chapter VIII.

232. M. Kasha, "Four great personalities of science: G. N. Lewis, J. Franck, R. S. Mulliken and A. Szent-Györgyi", *Pure & Appl. Chem.* **1990,** *62,* 1615.

233. A. C. Roosevelt, M. Lima da Costa, C. Lopes Machado, M. Michab, N. Mercier, H. Valladas, J. Feathers, W. Barnett, M. Imazio da Silveira, A. Henderson, J. Silva, B. Chernoff, D. S. Reese, J. A. Holman, N. Toth, K. Schick, "Paleoindian Cave Dwellers in the Amazon: The Peopling of the Americas", *Science,* **1996,** *272,* 373. See also evidence for age of the Chilean site Monte Verde, about 12,500 years. News story by Ann Gibbins, *Science,* **1997,** *275,* 1256. A recent article on the Monte Verde site in Chile appeared in *The Boston Globe,* March 17, 1997.

234. C. V. Haynes, Jr.; R. E. Reaner; W. P. Barse; with response by Roosevelt, *et al.* "Dating a Paleoindian Site in the Amazon in comparison with Clovis Culture," *Science,* **1997,** *275,* 1948. 235. Thor Heyerdahl *"Kon-Tiki; across the Pacific by Raft."* Rand McNally, Chicago, 1950.

236. An advertisement in "Chemical Heritage" Volume 13 No 2. Summer 1996 for a forthcoming book "Arrhenius: from Ionic Theory to the Greenhouse Effect" by Elizabeth Crawford, in preparation 1996.

237. W. A. E. McBryde, in "Nobel Laureates in Chemistry", L. K. James, Ed., American Chemical Society and the Chemical Heritage Foundation, 1993.

238. W. Heitler, "Wave Mechanics" 1945.

239. K. J. Laidler, "Lessons from the History of Chemistry", *Accts. Chem. Res.* **1995,** *28,* 187.

240. M. Kasha, personal communication.

241. T. Soderqvist, *Science,* **1996,** *207,* 1642; Review of "August and Marie Krogh", B. Schmidt-Nielsen, Oxford University press, New York, 1995.

236. William J. Locke, "The Joyous Adventures of Aristide Pujol."

237. This proclamation, as well as some information about the history of Paretchan's discovery and some earlier correspondence regarding Lewis's eminence are in *Chem. Eng. News,* **1993,** Nov. 1 1993, p25.

238. Congressional Record on Oct 25, 1993, S14287.

239. *Chemical and Engineering News,* **1993,** Nov., p 25.

INDEX

Abbott's Lagoon 74
Abegg 34
Academic Senate 52
Acids 33, 39, 63
Activity 15, 29, 30
Activity coefficients 30
Adams, G. P. 90
Alhambra 13
Alvarez, L. 48
American anthropology 48
Ammonium Nitrate 30
Anatomy of Sci. 17, 25, 29
Anfinson, C. B. 98
Argo, W. 16, 24, 37
Arrhenius Medal 64
Arrhenius, S. 7, 10
Atomic bomb 1
Atom and the Molecule 32
A-to-Zed School 78

Bacon, L. 69
Barbary coast 19
Bartlett, P. D. 78
Base 33, 39, 63
Berkeley, growth 19
    shops 19
    houses in 71
Biddle, H. C. 24, 28
Biegeleisen, J. 3, 36, 37, 57, 87
Bingham, E. C, 10
Blasdale, W. 24, 28
Bohemian Club 73
Bohemian Grove 73
Bohr, N. 79
Bohr atom 62
Booth, H. C. 24, 28
Bootlegger 75

Branch, G. 28, 32, 56, 69

Bray, W. 24, 28, 32, 69
Brazilian caves 48
Brest, explosion 30
Brewer, L. 2, 31, 40, 86
Bridges S. F. Bay 20
Brown, H. C. 94
Burr, A, Jr. 5
Burrs 5

California 3,4. 19
    Gas Chamber 23
    Rail access 19
California Institute of
Technology (Cal Tech) 20, 52
Calvin, Melvin 2, 3,27,28, 42, 43, 47, 64, 87
Cannon, W. 12, 69
Cech, T. 96
Chemical Warfare
service 24
Chemistry of stars 29
Chicago, Univ. Hon.
    degree 64
Chrysler 80, 83
Cigars 13
Civilization in America 3, 48
Cleveland (OH) 6
Clovis paradigm 48
Color 15, 29, 40, 43
Conductivity 31
Conservation of photons 46
Corey, E. J. 99
Cottrell, F. 20
Cram. D. J. 96

Crater Lake 83
Cummings, W. J. 24
Curl, R. F 95
Dago dinners 68
Darwin, C. 84
Davenport, D. 3, 87
Davy medal 64
Debye, P. 84
Debye-Hückel 32
Deep Springs School 77, 83
Deuterium 36
   compounds of 37
Dodge 80
Dominican Convent 77
Drama section 69
DuChamps, M. 91
Eastman, E. 28, 57
Educ. of children, elementary 76
Education, High School 77, 78
Einstein, A. 16, 46
Electron pair bond 32, 33
England 83
Eyring, H. 63

Faculty Club 68, 69
Fallen Leaf Lake 84
Fighting Bobs 13
Fission 1, 49
Ford, model T 80
Franklin medal 64
Freed, S. 64
Free Energy 31, 61
Freezing point depression 31
French, (language) 7
   legion of honor 25
Friends 69
Fugacity 15, 29, 30
Fukui, K. 99

Gay, W. 64, 69
Geography game 76
Georgia (USSR) 84
German language 7
Germany 10,11
Giauque, W. 28, 51, 64
Gibbs, J. W. 13, 32
Gibbs medal 64
Gibson, G. E. 28, 64, 69
81, 92
Glaciation 47
Goldsworthy, 69
Göttingen 11

Hammett equation 57
Hanson, Miss 75
Harvard Univ. 8, 9, 10, 11, 12
Head, Anna, school 77
Hearts (game) 68
Heavy water 36
Heitler 62
Herschbach, D. 92, 94
Heyerdahl, T. 49
Hildebrand, J. 3, 23, 24
28, 55, 58, 73
Hoffmann, R. 95
Home schooling 78
Hughes, E. W. 32
Hydrogen cyanide 25, 43

Ice age 4
Impertinent comment 55
Indian Acad. of Sciences 64
Industrial Chemistry 56
Ingold, C. K. 33
Inverness 21
   access to 72
   electricity in 76
   founding of 72
   house in 71
   location of 71

Inverness (cont,)
    reading aloud in   76
    reunion at   81
    winters in   80

Jensen, W. B.   2, 87
Joffe, W. L.   79
Jolly, W.   3, 43, 44, 51, 61

Karle, J.   97
Kasha, M. 2, 42, 43, 44,47, 57, 64, 87
Kennedy, E.   93
Kennedy, J. W.   28
Kilpatrick, J. E.   30
Kittredge, M.   51
Kohler, R. E.   34
Kon-Tiki   48
Koshland, D.   94, 96
Kossel   34
Kraus, C. A.   16
Kriegspiel   68
Krogh   65

Lachman, A.   3, 7, 17, 67
Linforth, I
Lafayette house   72
Laidler, K.   63
Langmuir, I.   33
Latimer, W.   28, 59
LeBel   43
Leipzig   11
Lewis, Frank   5
Lewis, George Gilbert   5
Lewis, G. N. (Gil)   82, 93
Lewis, Gilbert Newton
    appearance   90
    as camp cook   74
    contrast to Langmuir   73
    conversationalist   68, 90
    day in Massachusetts   93

Lewis, Gilbert Newton (cont.)
    diet   82
    driver   80
    dress   90
    Einstein, letter to   16
    faculty club room   80
    grandchildren   82
    high sch. sci. area   93
    illness   82
    limericks   90
    lunch   59, 68
    music taste   91
    puns   90
    suicide suggestion 43, 82
    view on rules   92
    Weymouth recog. day 93
    writing style   90

Lewis, Helen   5
Lewis, Jabez   5
Lewis, J. K   82
Lewis, Margery 6, 78, 80, 82
Lewis, Mary B. W.   5, 6, 75
Lewis, Mary (Polly)   5-8
Lewis, Mary (Sheldon) 71, 84
Lewis, R. N. 5, 71, 83, 84, 87
Lewis, R. P.   1
Libby, W.   28, 37, 52
Lingane, J. J.   28
Liverpool U. hon. deg.   64
Loewenberg, J.   69
Logan, M.   76

Madrid U. hon. deg.   64
Magnetism   34
Manila   11, 12, 15
Marsh, G.   69
Meyer, J. E.   32
Millikan, R.   11
MIT   13, 15
Monetary policy   46
Monte Verde   48
Morgan, W. C.   24, 28
Morse, H.   12, 69

Nat. Acad. of Sciences 52, 64
Navy   3,4
Nebraska   9

118

Nernst, W. 11, 61, 62
Neutron optics 46
Nichols medal 64
Nonpolar molecules 32, 33
Noyes, A. A. 13, 35, 52
Non-Euclidean geometry 44
Nuclear energy 48
Nuclear fission 48

Oakland 20
Observational sciences 45
Ocean beach 74
Octet 34
Oklahoma City explosion 31
Olah, G. 99
Olson, A. 28, 28, 29, 66
O'Neill, E. C. 24, 25, 28
Optical activity 45
Organic molecules 33, 44
Osmotic pressure 31
Ostwald, W. 10, 11
Oxford 83

Panama 19
Paramagnetism 34
Paretchan 3, 93, 94
Pasadena 35
Pauling, L. 2, 35, 52, 96
Pennsylvania, U. of Hon. Deg.64
Pepper, S. 69
Phillips Andover 10
Phillipines 12, 13
Phosphorescent State 42, 47
Pitzer, K. S. 2, 28, 33, 81, 87
Planck, M. 46
Plutonium 40
Point Reyes 74
    Nat. Seashore Park 72, 74
    Station 72
Poison oak 74
Polar molecules 33
Porter, C. W. 28, 83

Prall, M. 77
Prohibition 74

Quantum mechanics 1, 62

Randall, M.23, 28, 29, 30, 57
Rat house 24
Reaction rate theory 63
Redwoods 73
Relativity 1, 15, 44
Religion 78
Research conference 55
Research laboratory of
physical chemistry 13
Rice Univ. (inst.) 20, 30, 31
Richards, T. W. 9, 10, 64
67
Richards medal 64
Rollefson, G. 24, 28, 58
Rooseveldt, F. D. 75
Roy. Danish Academy 64
Roy. Institute of chem. 64
Royal Society 64
Ruben, S. 28
Rule of eight 33
Rutherford, Lord 94, 101

Sachse, H. 84
Saint Jean de Luz 83
San Francisco 19
    strikes 20
Sanscrit 81
Sausalito 72
Scholar-athlete 8
Schevill, R. 81
Scotia 73
Seaborg, G. T. 1, 2, 3, 13, 24
    28, 38, 39, 40, 58, 97
Seaborgium 40
Selby, M. (Lewis) 4
Selby, S. (Alcon) 4, 82
Servos, J. W. 2, 10, 87
Seventieth Birthday pub. 3
Sheldon, E. S. 71, 75

Sheldon, Mary H. (Lewis) 71, 77
Silliman Lectures 26, 90
Smith, A, 75
Smith, M. 99-100
Smoke 55
Social security 6
Soc. of arts and sciences
    medal 64
Stanford Univ. 20
State insurance 5
Stewart, T. D. 28
Stranges, A. N. 2, 87
Strong electrolytes 31

Tahiti 71
Taube, H 28, 52, 95
Telegraph 81
Tennis 81
Texas City explosion 30
Thermodynamics and the free
  energy of chemical substances
  also referred to as Lewis and
  Randall 15, 29, 30, 31
Thermodynamics 15, 16, 26, 29
    statistical 32
    generalized 32
    more fundamental 32
Throop institute 20
Tippett, J. E. 69
Tolman, E. C. 81
Tolman, R. C. 15, 25, 81
Tomales bay 71, 72
Tomales Point 72
Triplet State 41
Tritium 37

Ultimate rational units 46
Undergraduates education 58
University of California 1
    archives 1
    chemistry faculty 24, 27, 28
    chemistry PhDs 51
    at Davis 20

University of Calif. (cont)
    at Los Angeles 20
    my period 3
University of Nebraska 9
Univ. of Nebraska school 9
Univ.of Wisc. hon. degree 64
Urey, H. C. 36, 51
USSR trip 84
USSR Acad. memb. 64, 85

Valence and the structure of
atoms and molecules also
referred to as Valence 25, 29
    33, 34, 40
Valence and tautomerism 32
Van Duzen river 73
Vanny (S. Van Zandt) 75
Van't Hoff 43
Volga cruise 84

Wagon train 19
Washington, G. 6
Western investments 7
Weymouth 5, 7, 93, 94
White, N. 5
Wicht 12
Wilkinson, G. 98
Wilson, E. B. 17
Word games 76
World War I 24